Essentials of Economics

A BRIEF SURVEY OF PRINCIPLES AND POLICIES

Essentials of Economics

A BRIEF SURVEY OF PRINCIPLES AND POLICIES

by

FAUSTINO BALLVÉ

Translated from the Spanish and Edited by

ARTHUR GODDARD

THE FOUNDATION FOR
ECONOMIC EDUCATION, INC.
IRVINGTON-ON-HUDSON, NEW YORK 10533

The Foundation for Economic Education, Inc.
30 South Broadway
Irvington-on-Hudson, NY 10533

Publisher's Cataloging in Publication
(Prepared by Quality Books, Inc.)

Ballvé, Faustino.
    Essentials of economics : a brief survey of principles and policies / by Faustino Ballvé ; translated from the Spanish and edited by Arthur Goddard.   — 3rd English ed.
    p. cm.
    Includes index.
    English translation of Diez lecciones de economía.
    ISBN: 1-57246-069-5

    1. Economics.   I. Title.

HB178.3.B35 1997   330
                                    QBI97-40769

Library of Congress Catalog Card Number: 97-61136

First edition, Mexico, 1956; second edition, Mexico, 1961; third edition, Mexico, 1961. French translation, Paris, Sédif, 1957. Spanish editions in Buenos Aires, Argentina, and in Guatemala. English translation first printed in cloth edition by D. Van Nostrand Company, Inc., 1963; first FEE paperback edition, 1969. Second FEE edition published January 1994; second printing, March 1995; third FEE printing, August 1997.

Manufactured in the United States of America

PUBLISHER'S NOTE ON PRESENT PRINTING

This printing meets the longfelt need for a brief and authoritative primer of economics written in language easily understandable by the average intelligent person with no specialized knowledge of the subject. Without the distortions and oversimplifications that customarily mar popularized treatments of this science, the author has succeeded in presenting the essential teachings of economics in an eminently clear and readable form ideally suited to the needs of the citizen who seeks to acquaint himself with the knowledge necessary for a well-founded and rationally defensible opinion concerning the consequences of proposed policies that are currently the subject of controversy. Illustrated with apt historical references and buttressed with solid learning, this work is a rare combination of sound scholarship and pedagogic skill.

Within the compass of a few short chapters, the reader will find a synoptic survey of the fundamental principles of economics and will see them applied in the critique of popular fallacies, misunderstandings, and confusions. In spite of its conciseness, the text deals, always in a precise way, with a wide range of economic issues of interest and importance to every citizen of a democracy: monopolies, business cycles, unemployment, inflation and deflation, the gold standard, international trade, labor and wages, capital and profits, land and rents, nationalism, socialism, the planned economy, etc.

In the light of the teachings of economics, the author subjects to critical examination various proposals for governmental interference with the free market—e.g., price ceilings, minimum-wage laws, rent controls, import quotas, tariffs, subsidies, foreign-exchange controls, confiscatory taxation, expropriation measures, and land reform. The doctrines of the various "schools" of economic theory are succinctly presented and critically evaluated; and the scope of economic science is clearly delimited, first in the opening chapter, on what economics is about, and finally in the closing chapter, on what economics is not about.

The Foundation for Economic Education

The Translator's Preface

Elementary introductions to economic science comparable in clarity, authoritativeness, and simplicity to Sr. Ballvé's work are exceedingly rare, not only in Spanish but also in other languages. And, indeed, within a year of this book's publication, a French translation by M. Raoul Audoin made its appearance to fill the need of readers of that language in Continental Europe, where the book soon received the acclaim it deserved.

Certainly the same need exists in English and has existed for some time. There are, to be sure, a number of excellent treatises on economics, some of them rather voluminous, which expound the subject with an exhaustiveness that should satisfy the most demanding student. But when one looks for simpler and briefer presentations, designed, not for specialists, but for the average educated person who seeks enlightenment in regard to the economic questions underlying the great issues of our day, there is little to be found that is altogether satisfactory. No doubt those who have taken the pains to acquire a thorough knowledge of economics may say that there really is no substitute for the consummate understandings that only the study of the works of the masters in this field can provide; anything else is necessarily superficial at best and is likely to be open to sophisticated criticism. This much may be granted. But the gap between the erudition of the scholars—a relatively small group, whose primary influence is in the classroom and the lecture hall—and the ignorance, not to say prejudices, of even otherwise well-educated men and women who have not specialized in economic science, has not been left a vacuum. There is no dearth of pamphlets and popular books in which inveterate errors and fallacies long since refuted continue to be given currency. As for the textbooks used in the secondary schools and the colleges, besides being often dull and pedantic, they fail, in many instances, to reflect the present state of economic science, deal with much that is strictly irrelevant to it, and are, in any case, unsuited to the requirements of the citizen who wishes to inform himself accurately concerning the essentials of that subject so that he may have a well-founded, rationally defensible opinion concerning the consequences to be expected from the various proposed policies open to his choice in his capacity as a voter in a democracy.

It was chiefly for this type of reader that the "ten lessons in economics" here presented were intended. The peculiar merit of this book is its combination of brevity, readability, and accuracy. Here the reader will find, within the compass of a few short chapters, a synoptic survey of the essential principles of economics and an application of them in the critique of popular doctrines and policies, the whole illustrated with apt historical references and supported by solid learning. This unusual blend of pedagogic skill and sound scholarship gives the work its unique character and makes it ideally suited to fill a need that has, up to now, been left, for the most part, unsatisfied. Its translation into English will have been justified if it helps to clear up some of the grave misunderstandings and confusion that infect much of the popular discussion of economic questions and to correct the faulty opinions that currently constitute the main obstacle to the diffusion of prosperity and well-being.

The English version is based, for the most part, on the original Spanish-language edition, but it takes account also of some of the substantive changes that, as we learn from M. Pierre Lhoste Lachaume's preface to the French translation, were introduced into the text of the latter at his suggestion. To be sure, not all the additions, deletions, emendations, and rearrangements made in the French version have been incorporated into the English text, for in some cases they appear to have been made—as the editor frankly admitted—chiefly in the interest of adapting the book to the concerns of the French public or of bringing certain points into sharper relief in the light of contemporary European conditions. However, in view of Sr.

Ballvé's express statement, in the foreword he wrote for the French translation, of his approval of the revised text, the latter has been followed here wherever it seemed to represent an improvement, in vigor and consistency of expression, over the Spanish original.

Arthur Goddard

Table of Contents

1

What Is Economics About?

Economic activity. Economic thought. Xenophon, Aristotle, Rome, St. Thomas, Oresmius, Biel, Erasmus, Luther, Calvin. Mercantilism. The physiocrats. Adam Smith and the classical school. Nationalism. The Historical School. Socialism. The controlled economy. The Austrian School. The Mathematical School. The Critical School. The domain of the economic: action chosen by man in the market.

As far back as we go in our study of the way mankind has lived, from the earliest reaches of recorded history and even from the times of the prehistoric monuments studied by archeology, we find men applying their labor to the resources of Nature in order to satisfy their needs. That is to say, we find them producing —even if only by bagging game or catching fish or gathering from fields and forests the wood and the wild fruits they found growing there, transporting these to the place where they were to be consumed, and then treating them as marketable commodities—and we find them exchanging their produce with other men, whether directly by barter or indirectly through the medium of a neutral commodity, viz., money. We find them, too, competing in offer and demand, according to the conditions of scarcity or abundance in the supply of specific goods, and exercising the right of choice—the producer producing what he expects will yield him the greatest profit, and the consumer buying what seems to him cheapest and most suitable to his needs. We also

1

find them holding on to goods or money, sometimes with the object of securing a greater advantage later, sometimes with that of building up a reserve for hard times. We find those in possession of goods or money lending, for some consideration, what they could spare to those in urgent need of it, and we find different people banding together for production or consumption.

All these human activities, consisting in the exercise of individual initiative and of the faculty of choice for the satisfaction of wants and the improvement of what we call today the standard of living, are, in a more or less primitive and undeveloped form, as old as mankind. Their modern forms are every day being extended from the advanced to the backward countries at the same time that their primitive forms persist into the present day. Indeed, the latter are still current among civilized peoples, as we see in the recrudescence of barter during and after the war even among nations as enlightened as France, Germany, and the United States.[1]

From the earliest times, too, this manifestation of human activity has engaged the minds of scholars and thinkers. To go no further back than the days of ancient Greece,[2] Plato concerned himself with the division of labor and of the various occupations; Xenophon dealt with the increase in rents in Attica and formulated a theory of money; Aristotle spoke of the *chrematistic* occupations, expressed the hope that slave labor might be replaced by machinery, and anticipated the distinction that Adam Smith was to make twenty-two centuries later between value in use and value in exchange. Rome made the protection of agriculture an economic policy—one that was supported in the Middle Ages by the Catholic Church's condemnation of trade, its prohibition on the charging of interest, which it characterized as usury, its repudiation of value in exchange, and its refusal to accept, as the basis for prices, anything but value in use.

St. Thomas Aquinas advocated a kind of communism that was later, from 1610 to 1766, to be practiced by the Jesuits of Paraguay. The French bishop Nicholas Oresmius published a treatise on money, and Gabriel Biel of Württemberg made investigations into the nature of money and the formation of prices.

Humanism, with Erasmus, esteemed commerce as honorable. Martin Luther, the founder of Protestantism, postulated that "man was born to work," studied the division of labor, and stressed the importance and utility of trade, recommending the free market even though he continued to condemn "usury." On this last point Calvin disagreed with Luther and was, besides, the first to advocate the intervention of the state in economic life—an intervention that already existed in his age and, to a greater or lesser degree, has always existed and in the last thirty years has been considered as an economic panacea.

The establishment of absolute monarchies in the sixteenth and seventeenth centuries and the rise of modern nations imbued with an ardent and youthful spirit of nationalism produced at the same time a control over economic activity and a theoretical justification of that control that is known historically as *mercantilism*. Its fundamental principles, of which those of the present age, aptly called *neomercantilist*, remind us, are: the direction of economic life by the public authorities, the consideration of money as true wealth, a concern with a favorable balance of payments with the object of obtaining more money in international exchange, the protection of industry for the purpose of having articles of export in order to bring money into the country, a system of subsidies and privileges for exporters and for industries producing for export or avoiding imports, an increase in the population in order to augment the productive forces of the domestic economy, competition with and isolation of foreigners by means of tariff barriers, and, above all, the belief that the prosperity of one country is possible only at the expense of the others.

These were the principles that inspired the regulation of economic life by the omnipotent governments of the sixteenth to the eighteenth century and were developed, albeit with considerable differences of detail, by Serra, Broggia, and Genovesi in Italy; by Francis Bacon (Lord Verulam), Thomas Mun, Child, and Temple in England (while Sir Walter Raleigh attributed the economic superiority of Holland to its greater economic freedom); by Melon and Forbonnais in France; by Klock, Seckendorff, Becher, and Baron von Schoeder in Germany; and by Luis Ortiz, Moncada, Damián de Olivares, Gracián Serran, Jerónimo Ustariz, and Bernardo de Ulloa in Spain. The statesman who has come to be regarded as the most representative historical exemplar of this tendency is Colbert, the minister of Louis XIV.

The mercantilist system led to disastrous consequences; for the fragmentation of economic and political groups ended by strangulating general economic life and producing internal misery and external war. The example of Holland led Queen Elizabeth of England to grant greater freedom to commerce and to reduce the importance of the guilds. Incipient liberalism, supported by the doctrine of natural law, immediately inspired a critique of the whole mercantilist system and a scientific trend in the opposite direction that is known as the *physiocratic* school. Its initiators were Pierre de Boisguillebert, Marshal Vauban, and, above all, Quesnay, personal physician to Louis XV. They were followed by Vincent Gournay, the elder Mirabeau, and, to some extent, the celebrated statesman Turgot.

As its name indicates, this doctrine was founded on the principle that there are *natural laws* of economic life that operate automatically. The evils of mercantilism come from interference with these laws on the part of the state. Hence, it is advisable to abstain from all regulation of economic activity and to leave it entirely to individual initiative. This principle Gournay reduced to the celebrated phrase: *laissez faire, laissez passer.*

The physiocratic doctrine, in so far as it was a reaction against mercantilism, found propitious soil in England. There neither the mercantilist worship of money nor the veneration of agriculture as the sole foundation of national wealth, which the physiocrats had taken over from the canonists, had ever completely prevailed. However, the English did not content themselves with the mere affirmation of the existence of natural laws with whose operation the state ought not to interfere, but wanted to investigate these laws and determine what they are; and thus they gave the world the so-called *classical school* of economics. The way was opened by Hutcheson and David Hume, who in turn influenced Adam Smith, the author of the first treatise on economics properly so called, entitled *Inquiry into the Nature and Causes of the Wealth of Nations* (1776). In England David Ricardo and, to a certain extent, both James Mill and his son John, in France Jean-Baptiste Say and Frédéric Bastiat, and in Germany Henry and J. H. von Thünen, Rau, Hermann, and Nebenius took their inspiration from Smith.

A discordant note was struck in England by Robert Malthus, an Anglican curate, with his theory that population tends to increase faster than the means of subsistence. He advised recourse to measures designed to avoid the disastrous consequences of simply allowing the laws of nature to run their course. In the United States the classical doctrine was embraced by Franklin and Hamilton (who was, notwithstanding, a protectionist). The chief exponents in Spain were José Alonso Ortiz, who translated Smith's work and wrote a commentary on it, and Alvaro Flores Estrada, who nevertheless also initiated the movement of agrarian reform that almost a century later was to bring renown to the American Henry George.

The apogee of the classical school coincided with the fabulous increase in production and international exchange consequent upon the introduction of machinery (the Industrial Revolution) [3] and the improvement of communications. But three circumstances brought the classical doctrine into disrepute. The first was the discovery that what had been taken for laws presumably deducible from the observation of economic phenomena in a limited geographical area (England and France in particular), and about which there was considerable disagreement among the adherents of the classical school, were not really laws at all, but mere regularities that, when treated as infallible laws, often failed in their application. The second was the inferior competitive position in which the younger countries, especially Germany and the United States, felt themselves to be on the world market. The third was the general opinion, more or less well founded, but disseminated by propaganda and unreflectingly accepted by the intellectuals and the middle class, that the lower classes and especially the workers were not benefiting from the material progress engendered by free enterprise.

Hence arose three countermovements: *nationalist* protectionism, launched in Germany by Frederick List, of which the last and most eminent representative was Adolf Wagner (a policy advocated in the United States by Henry Carey and in England by the elder Chamberlain and the adherents of the *tariff-reform* movement); *socialism* in its diverse forms, of which the most prominent was the so-called "scientific socialism" of Karl Marx and Frederick Engels; and the so-called *Historical School* (Bruno Hildebrand, Knies, Roscher, Schmoller), itself a reflection of both romanticism and the positivism of Auguste Comte, according to which every country has its particular economy corresponding to its conditions and traditions and serving the national interest rather than that of the individual. These three trends of thought, including the socialist, which originally had a cosmopolitan character, tended toward acceptance of the myth of national wealth, to which they subordinated that of the individual, and in whose defense they affirmed that all measures are legitimate in the name of "sacred egoism."

It is curious to note that these doctrines, which called themselves "modern," and which we shall study in detail later, in spite of their professed opposition to classical liberalism, all (including Marxian socialism) followed in its footsteps and are not so much its adversaries as its offspring. In the first place, they conceive of the theme of economics, not as man's universal struggle for well-being, but as national, *political* economy. Thus, quite recently, Professor Fuchs, of Germany, has defined political economy [4] as "the study of the economy of a people" and considered its function to be that of the "ever increasing support and ever more perfect satisfaction of the necessities of a growing population in a given territory." In the second place, these doctrines do not grasp the economy in its unity and totality, but continue to treat distribution and consumption separately and without any connection, as if they were independent entities and not merely parts of a general process. In the third place, they persist in the belief in the existence of laws that control the economic process independently of the will of man. Thus, Marx himself—contrary to all previous as well as all subsequent experience—conceived of the historical course of economic development as presided over by the great law of the concentration of capital, by virtue of which wealth is every day becoming concentrated in fewer hands while the "army of the proletariat" increases, until the inevitable moment comes when "the expropriators will be expropriated."

It did not occur to the exponents of these doctrines that economic events are not inevitable, but the product of man's free will; that production, distribution, and consumption are simply different aspects of a single economic process; that, in spite of nationalistic and isolationist experiments, the economy of the whole world constitutes a unified totality; or, finally, that no law or government has succeeded or indeed can succeed in preventing every man from striving after his own and his loved ones' earthly well-being in the way he considers most suitable by making use of his faculty of free choice (the natural corollary of his liberty, as we see in the activities of smugglers in contravention of the laws limiting international trade and in the so-called "black market" in violation of the legal restrictions on domestic commerce).

These three "modern" tendencies—distrust of individual initiative, exacerbated nationalism (called *chauvinism* after the ultranationalist French Bonapartist Chauvin), and socialism—were, for all practical purposes, combined, at the end of the nineteenth century and the beginning of the twentieth, in *neomercantilism*. This began in the Germany of Bismarck and in the United States, spread by reaction to England, France, and other countries, produced the two world wars, and destroyed the international division of labor. Christened in Germany in 1920 the "planned economy" *(Planwirtschaft)* and later everywhere called the "controlled economy," under the pretext of defending national interests against foreign competition and the humbler classes against domestic oppression, it has enthroned the *omnipotent state* wherever it has gained a foothold and has forced democracy and liberty, whose universal victory was once thought to have been finally assured, into retreat.

But the love of liberty is no less imperishable than the love of knowledge, that is, the unprejudiced and fearless quest for truth. It was this strictly scientific spirit that inspired Carl Menger, around 1870, to undertake a revision of the prevailing economic doctrines with the object of placing economics on a truly scientific foundation.

Menger, a Viennese professor of economics, formulated the theory of *marginal utility (Grenznutztheorie)* [5] almost at the same time as Stanley Jevons did in England and Léon Walras in France. From it issued two distinct currents of thought: the Mathematical School and the so-called "Austrian" School represented by Menger himself, Böhm-Bawerk, Wieser, and others, and at present by Ludwig von Mises, author of *Human Action*,[6] and his pupil, Friedrich von Hayek, author of the famous book entitled *The Road to Serfdom*.[7] Both are today professors in the United States with an increasingly large number of disciples, and supporting their position is the American economist Henry Hazlitt, author of the famous *Economics in One Lesson*.[8]

The Mathematical School, which reached its height in the work of the French economist Cournot, has given rise to two divergent streams of thought: one branch, starting with Walras, Pareto, and Pantaleoni, has developed so-called "econometrics," which professes to be able to attain complete exactitude in economic calculation and is the chief bulwark of the ideology of central economic planning at the present time;[9] while the other, starting with the English economist Marshall, uses mathematics solely as a graphic means of expressing economic doctrines without pretending in any way to have made of economics an "exact science." Among these mathematical economists should be mentioned John Bates Clark and Irving Fisher.

Walter Eucken and Wilhelm Röpke, both German (although the latter has done most of his work in Egypt and Switzerland), represent a liberal, nonmathematical tendency. In France, which has maintained a high rank in economic science, the liberal movement is represented by such eminent figures as Charles

Gide, Rist, and, more recently, Jacques Rueff, Louis Baudin, Pierre Lhoste-Lachaume, and many others.

Several other contemporary schools of economic thought could be mentioned, like that of "dynamic" economics, which originated in the Scandinavian countries, and of which Schumpeter (an Austrian who died recently in the United States) is a representative; but they have no definite form or any significant influence. On the other hand, it is noteworthy that Ludwig von Mises and his disciples represent a considerable advance over their predecessors of the so-called "Austrian" School; in fact, they can be considered as the founders of an altogether new school that could well be called "critical."

According to this strictly scientific new school of thought, *the economic domain is constituted by human action directed toward the satisfaction of wants by the exercise of the power of choice. Economics is, accordingly, the study of this economic activity on the part of man.* It is not concerned with philosophical or moral problems, since *economic science is not adjudicative, but descriptive.* Nor, by the same token, does economics deal with political problems, since *the economist does not give advice:* he confines himself strictly to explicating the nature of economic activity, leaving it to the good sense of the statesman and the citizen in general to draw from this knowledge whatever consequences may recommend themselves. Finally, economics pays no attention to historical problems, since *history tells us*—and therein it can serve as an adjunct to political science—*only what has been,* but not what is, much less what will be. Nor can statistics, which refers only to past events, be anything more than an adjunct to history.

It is thus that we arrive at the unique domain that constitutes the true subject matter of economic science. Because economic activity takes place in time and space, it involves concurrences, contrarieties, and concatenations of events. These *external variations* are the proper subject matter of *history* and of *economic geography.* But behind these variations reflection discovers (though not by a process of mere observation and comparison) certain uniform and invariant aspects of man's economic activity, of which we have cited a few examples at the beginning of this chapter. These *general and constant forms* of man's economic activity *constitute the subject matter of economic science,* while its variations in time and space constitute the field proper to geography and history.

Having thus set forth, in necessarily brief form, the nature and history of economics, and the true character of its subject matter, we propose to take up in turn, in the nine succeeding chapters, the study of the various topics into which this subject can be broken down, the questions to which they give rise, as well as the various solutions that have been suggested to present-day economic problems, and to criticize these from the scientific point of view. The topics of these chapters will be: (2) the market (the division of labor, competition, value, and price); (3) the role of the entrepreneur and economic calculation; (4) capital, labor, and wages; (5) money, credit, and interest; (6) monopolies, crises, and unemployment; (7) international trade; (8) nationalism and socialism; (9) the controlled economy; and (10) what economics is *not* about.

2

The Market

The autistic and the co-operative economy. The division of labor, exchange, and the market. Commerce and trade. The sovereignty of the consumer. Monopoly, economic dictatorship, and the black market.

Man is incapable of satisfying all his wants by his own unaided efforts. Individual autarky, i.e., a completely autistic, self-sufficient economy, is impossible. It is a kind of economy that is encountered only in utopias like that of Robinson Crusoe, but never in the actual life of man.

Men need to have recourse to other men to obtain the goods and services they lack, in exchange for other goods and services that they can offer.

Hence resulted the household economy of the individual family, in which the man hunted or fished and at the same time protected the members of his family against danger. They, *in exchange*, took care of hearth and home, prepared the meals, gathered the wild fruits they found growing in the forests, and fashioned primitive garments. Each individual exchanged goods and services with another.

The basis of the *co-operative economy* thereby achieved was the *division of labor*.

There are some who think this a modern innovation. But it is not. It has always been a constant feature of economic activity.

11

Professor von Mises rightly says in his book *Human Action:* "The exchange relation is the fundamental social relation." [1]

The exchange relation—or, more simply, in economic terms, *exchange*—takes place in the *market.* The family that has eggs to spare exchanges them for meat with another family that needs eggs and has an excess of meat. But this is not enough. Sometimes a family that has eggs and needs meat finds that its neighbor has only fish to spare, which can then be exchanged for meat.

These relations gradually grow more complicated, and it becomes more convenient to go to a public market place to offer for sale whatever one has in superfluity in exchange for what one lacks, whether by direct barter or in an indirect way.

The exchange of commodities was facilitated with the invention of *money.* At first this appeared in a primitive form, until it developed into the coined money that we all know and use. Then goods and services were exchanged for money, or vice versa.

Exchange or *commerce* ceased to be local and spread between one town and another until it became international.

Everything mentioned so far, from the exchange of meat for eggs between neighboring families to international trade, constitutes the *market,* the pivot around which all of economic life revolves. The market is the foundation of every economy.

In the market things are exchanged against things or against services, services against services, or services or things against money. Whatever is susceptible of exchange in the market constitutes a *commodity.*

From the strictly economic point of view, anything and everything that is exchanged must be classified as a commodity. Whoever goes to the market is in quest of an exchange that will satisfy a want, that is to say, something that will serve to render his life more agreeable. Hence, instead of the word "merchandise," * English usage prefers the word "commodity" ** in this

* [In Spanish, *mercancía* or *mercadería*, related etymologically to the word for "market" (*mercado*), as the English word "merchandise" is related to the French word for "market" (*marché*).—TRANSLATOR.]

** [*Comodidad* in Spanish means "comfort," "utility," "convenience," "advantage." —TRANSLATOR.]

context to refer to whatever is susceptible of exchange, whether goods or services. A thing has *value* when it is a commodity and is capable of being exchanged in the market.

Value always expresses a judgment of the estimation in which something is held, because a thing has a value if and only in so far as it is wanted or desired. For example, a millionaire can buy a diamond for a hundred thousand dollars and find himself dying of thirst in the desert and unable to obtain even a glass of water in exchange for his diamond, which there lacks all value.

It is said, especially by the mathematical economists, that the value of a thing increases as it becomes scarcer. But this is by no means certain, for it can happen that a thing may become scarcer every day and yet have no value at all because nobody wants it. Horse-drawn carriages have become very scarce nowadays, and yet nobody wants them. They have no value at all, or hardly any. Nonetheless, only those things are *economic goods* that we lack and long to have, not *free goods* that are in the reach of all, like the air that we breathe.

The distinction between *value in use* and *value in exchange* was first made by Aristotle, was adopted by the canonists, and was later developed by the classical economists. *Value in use* is the utility that a thing has *in itself*. *Value in exchange* is what it will fetch in the market. It has been contended, as the canonists did in an earlier day, that it is morally wrong to take advantage of a thing's scarcity in order to obtain more in exchange for it than its value in use.

However, this distinction is untenable. For even though it is true that an automobile generally has more value than a needle, it is altogether possible that in a concrete case (depending on time and circumstances) the contrary could occur. A tailor who is in want of a needle cannot sew with an automobile, and in places where gasoline is not to be had, automobiles have no value at all. Besides, how many needles is an automobile worth? It is difficult—or rather, impossible—to say definitely, because the utility of each varies according to time and place, and, in the last analysis, only the prices quoted in the market tell us the relation of the *value in exchange* between two commodities. Therefore, it is not possible to establish a quantitative relation of values according to the *value in use* of the automobile and of the needle. All that is possible is a qualitative estimation of a general character, because an automobile is generally considered more valuable than a needle, but this need not always be the case, nor does this difference in value admit of being expressed in quantitative terms.

For that matter, a thing's *value in use* is not constant either, because some new invention or discovery, or simply a change in prevailing tastes, can diminish it or even wipe it out entirely. Our mothers kept in their wardrobes dresses and hats that in their day had a considerable value in use and today have none at all. On the other hand, the hats and dresses of the present, far more simple, but more in fashion, do have value.

Penicillin reduced the value in use of many medicines, but others, like streptomycin, terramycin, and chloromycin, have diminished the value in use of penicillin. For these reasons the concept of value in use, even though it has some basis in fact, serves no purpose in economics.

An attempt has also been made to find in *labor* a measure of the *value* of things. This results from insistence on determining the "just" value of things, thereby confounding an economic question with a moral question that has nothing to do with it. The attempt has been made in two ways. In the early days of classical economics it was said that since things are the fruits of human labor expended in the utilization or transformation of natural resources, their value ought to be measured in terms of the labor involved in their production. From this the socialists derived their demand that the workers receive the *whole proceeds of their labor,* from which, it was charged, the capitalists retain a *surplus value* consisting of that part of the proceeds of labor which is not indispensable for the bare subsistence of the laborer.

The classical economists were not long in observing that, in the first place, the difficulty of the calculation made it practically impossible to take the labor involved in production as the measure of the value of the product, and, besides, the labor required for the production of a thing varies according to place and time, depending on the skill of the managers and workers at a given moment and on the extent to which techniques and means of production are perfected during the course of the years. Hence, they proposed measuring the value of things, not by the labor that they *cost the producer,* but by the labor they *saved the purchaser.* But this criterion, too, proved impracticable because of the difficulty of determining how much labor the purchase of a thing actually saved the buyer in general. The purchase of a delivery wagon will effect a definite saving for a confectionery store and a different amount for a hosiery factory or a radio store. Should each one of them, then, pay a different price?

Must we therefore revert, for our criterion of value, not to the labor saved the purchaser, but to the labor involved in production? Or, to avoid these problems, is the value of each thing to be fixed by the average amount of labor that it presumably cost its various producers? But on what are we to base this average cost? And who is to fix it? The government? Is the price we are to pay for things to be set by the arbitrary decree of the governmental authorities, when they have no more basis than anyone else for arriving at an objective valuation? This is precisely what is done in Russia today, and the result is that when the government sets on any commodity a price that is cheap in the estimation of the consumers, the latter hasten to purchase it until the existing supply is exhausted, and then the government is obliged to raise the price. Contrariwise, when the price that the government sets for a commodity seems dear to the consumer, he abstains from purchasing it, and the commodity remains indefinitely on the shelves as an unsold item of inventory, immobilizing capital and running the risk of deteriorating. Then the government, to extricate itself, is obliged to lower the price. In other words, *supply and demand* come into play even in a nationalized economy.

Supply and demand constitute the mechanism of the market

that determines *prices,* which are the value of goods and services expressed in terms of another, neutral commodity, viz., *money.* These prices are formed by *competition* in the market, not only among those who offer to sell goods and services, but also among those seeking to buy them. When a commodity is in abundant supply and is difficult to sell, the vendors, to avoid immobilizing the capital it represents and running the risk of its depreciation through spoilage or a change in the tastes of the consumers, lower prices and compete with one another to make a sale. When, on the contrary, an article is scarce and is in public demand, people are prepared to pay higher prices in order to obtain it, and competition arises among those seeking to purchase it. However, the latter case is rather rare. Generally it is the sellers who compete and lower their prices in order to satisfy the buyers.

Hence it has been said that free trade or the free market means *the sovereignty of the consumer.* And so effective, so necessary, so ineluctable is this sovereignty that, as we have just had occasion to observe, not even the communist economy can suppress it completely. And as the consumer is the public in general, without distinction of rank or fortune, the free market is the most obvious expression of the sovereignty of the people and the best guarantee of democracy. Individual guarantees stated in writing in the constitution are of no use to a nation if it is not the people, but a third party, whether government or trade-union, that fixes prices and wages and determines what is to be produced and what is to be sold; for in that case the people, in being deprived of their *right of free choice* in the market, i.e., their right to assign everything the rank and the value it suits them to give it, from being sovereign are reduced to the status of slaves. Control of the market by the governmental authorities is the instrument of the modern dictatorships, much less cruel in appearance, much less spectacular, but far more effective than the police and resort to naked force.

In clarification of the foregoing, we can conclude with the following remarks:

1. *Nothing has value in itself.* The consumer confers value

on it by seeking to acquire it. Hence, the value of a thing is never objective, but always subjective.

2. The monetary *price* of a thing is not the *measure* of its value, but only an expression of it. To say that a cow is worth two hundred dollars is nothing else than to say that it is worth twenty ewes or a sewing machine.

3. It is an error to believe that he who buys a thing wishes to give for it an *equivalent* value or that he who pays two hundred dollars for a cow thinks that a cow has the same value as two hundred dollars, or vice versa. In the market the buyer as well as the seller *gives less than he gets*. Whoever pays two hundred dollars for a cow does so because for him the cow that he gets is worth more than the sum that he gives for it, and whoever sells a cow for two hundred dollars does so because for him that sum is worth more than the cow. If this were not so, no exchange would take place: each one of them would keep what he already has.

4. *The sovereignty of the consumer does not mean the tyranny of the consumer.* The resistance of the latter, aided by the competition among the sellers, succeeds in keeping prices at a low level that nevertheless allows a margin for the subsistence of those who have participated in the production of the merchandise and its transportation to the market, such as the entrepreneur, the capitalist, the technicians, the workers, and the merchants. If, in spite of this, the consumer still continues to hold back, then prices do not fall any further, because nobody wants to make a gift of his possessions or his labor; what happens is that the merchandise in question ceases to be produced and sold and disappears from the market. But if it is a commodity that the consumer considers useful, he will give up his resistance and relax his pressure on the producer.

5. Neither does the free market involve the *dictatorship of the producer* or of the merchant. For if the producer or the tradesman dealing in a particular commodity, or all the producers joined together, demand in the market excessive prices because they are the only ones who have such merchandise (i.e., if they

constitute a monopoly), then not only does the consumer abstain from buying and forgo that commodity, replacing it with some substitute ("Better some of a pudding than none of a pie"),* but other, less avaricious suppliers and businessmen produce it and offer it for sale at a lower price. Thus, the price level is necessarily one that both buyer and seller find equally tolerable.

6. *Economic dictatorship* arises when production and trade are withdrawn from the mechanism of the market by the action of the governmental authorities. Then neither the consumer nor the seller is sovereign, but only the dictatorship of the bureaucracy over both, even though this is not one hundred per cent effective, as we have already seen in the case of Russia. The market continues to function, nonetheless, albeit in clandestine form (the black market); but in any case, economic dictatorship deprives the people of their liberty and well-being.

* [The sense of the Spanish proverb here cited by the author is rendered with perhaps greater literalness by its Scottish equivalent: "Bannocks are better nor nae kind o' bread."—TRANSLATOR.]

3

The Role of the Entrepreneur

Entrepreneur and consumer. Economic calculation. The data of the market. Factors and means of production. Comparative cost. Marginal utility. Diminishing returns. The time factor. Risk.

We have seen that the market is the pivot around which the whole of economic life revolves. We can say just as well that the market revolves around the entrepreneur.

The *entrepreneur* is the person, natural or juristic (i.e., individual or collective), who enters the market with the object of making a profit, that is to say, of getting more than he gives. In this sense, all those who go to the market are entrepreneurs, buyers as well as sellers, since anyone who buys a cow for two hundred dollars does so because he considers that, for him, the cow is worth more than the money he pays for it. Otherwise he would keep his two hundred dollars. However, in economics one who enters the market in order to obtain what he needs for his own use is not called an entrepreneur, but a *consumer*. Strictly speaking, the entrepreneur is anyone who goes to the market to sell or anyone who goes to the market to buy, not for his own consumption, but to resell what he has bought.

The entrepreneur aims at making a profit, and to this end he is obliged to resort to appropriate means. He thus has to exercise his power of choice twice: he has to choose the end, and he has to choose the means of attaining it. For both he has to make

19

use of his judgment, of his own powers of reasoning. This is called *economic calculation*.

The first thing that must be done by whoever considers himself an entrepreneur and desires to enter the market to offer for sale something that will yield him a profit is to decide on the kind of thing he is going to trade in. It may be something entirely produced by him, or something he has transformed from what it was when he acquired it; or it may simply be in the same physical condition as it was when he got it, but improved in his estimation by his having kept it until the consumer needed it or by his having transported it from where it was not useful to where it is; or perhaps he has just broken it up or accumulated it in quantities acceptable to the consumer. To come to such a decision, he must study the market, that is to say, he will have to be guided by what in economics are called *the data of the market*. He has to take into account what is already in abundant supply in the market and what therefore it is not advisable to offer for sale; what is in short supply and consequently will easily find ready purchasers; what the qualities are that are predominantly in demand; whether it is expedient to offer one quality or another; and finally, what the future *prospects* of the market are, i.e., what promises to prove profitable, not now, but when he enters the market and even after that. This applies as much to goods as to services: nobody will undertake today to sell things that are out of fashion, nor will anybody offer the services of an ostler on a modern automobile highway. It is rather to be supposed that at the present moment some entrepreneur is calmly preparing to enter a business connected with the peaceful uses of atomic energy.

Having chosen the end, i.e., the kind of speculation he is going to embark on, the entrepreneur has next to concern himself with the means by which he is to carry out his project. These are called, in general, *means of production*, even though they may not involve the production of material things, but simply the rendering of services. A producer is not only one who makes shoes; he is also one who distributes them, one who transports them. All produce, in the last analysis, *commodities*; that is to say, they accommodate the consumer by satisfying his needs and desires.

These means of production can be divided into two categories: the *factors of production* and the *techniques of production*.

The factors of production are essentially *capital* and *labor*. The former is divided into fixed and circulating capital. *Fixed capital* consists of land, buildings, machinery, tools, means of transport, and other permanent factors needed to produce the goods and services that the entrepreneur will offer for sale in the market. For a textile factory, these would be the looms and other machines needed in the various stages of preparing the yarn, processing it, and producing the finished cloth. For a distributor, they would include warehouses for storing the merchandise, as well as scales for weighing it, packing materials, and other apparatus to enable him to distribute his wares. An enterprise engaged in journalism must invest in facilities for gathering the news, whether by cable or wireless, as well as typewriters, duplicating machines of all kinds, etc., in its various branch offices; and the fixed capital of the agriculturist consists of the soil, grist mills, olive presses, tractors, and ploughs.

Circulating capital is the money needed for the purchase of the raw materials, lubricants, composts, seeds, wages and salaries, rent, light, etc., that enable the entrepreneur to go on producing and to keep his business in operation. As part of the costs of production, this is a factor that enters into the sales price of the product.

Labor consists in the services of all those engaged in the enterprise, beginning with the entrepreneur himself—who, with the factors already mentioned, arranges for the production of the goods or services that are to be offered for sale in the market —from the highest ranks of intellectual workers down to the humblest hired hands.

Besides the material means or factors of production, the entrepreneur has to provide himself with *technical* means, choosing those that he considers to be the most adequate. There are diverse methods of producing textiles, iron or steel, chemical or pharmaceutical products, etc. Each has its advantages and its disadvantages, and he has to select the one that is most appropriate for his purpose, taking into account the wants he wishes to satisfy, the processes used by his competitors, the costs involved in the use of each method, and the corresponding profit to be expected from its employment, etc., etc. In certain cases the entrepreneur may himself be the inventor of a technical process for which he obtained a *patent,* or he may have obtained from another inventor such a patent or a trade-mark or a design or an industrial model of an earlier producer or of a foreign producer who has granted him, for a period of time, an *exclusive* license to produce or to distribute the commodity in question.

But this is not all. Among the technical problems that the entrepreneur has to resolve are the provision of raw materials and the system of production, i.e., whether to undertake the complete process of turning the raw material into the finished product or to begin with half-finished goods, whether to hire labor at a fixed wage or to pay on a piecework basis, etc. Also very important are the extent of the enterprise and of the means that the entrepreneur has at his disposal, the prospects of the market, and, above all, the net *return* yielded by his industrial unit. All of this calculation he will do in the light of his own knowledge or that of people paid by him to provide expert mechanical, chemical, technical, industrial, or commercial information, and also on the basis of the teachings of economic experience that are comprehended under the rubric of *economic geography, economic history,* and *statistics.*

Within this body of knowledge needed by the entrepreneur in order to exercise his power of choice in launching and managing his enterprise are included what are commonly called economic laws. Among the latter should be mentioned chiefly *the law of comparative cost, the law of marginal utility,* and *the law of diminishing returns.*

According to *the law of comparative cost,* more recently known as the law of association, as formulated by the classical economist David Ricardo, in view of the greater or lesser extent of industrial progress of different countries, if, for example, producer A needs three hours to produce commodity X and two hours to produce commodity Y, while producer B (in a country in a less advanced state of industrial development) needs five and four hours respectively, it is advantageous for all concerned for A to produce only commodity Y and for B to produce only commodity X, for in that case each of them will produce a greater quantity in the same number of hours, and the two together will produce more of both commodities than if each had undertaken to produce them both. This is the so-called law of association or law of comparative cost, a corollary of the law of the division of labor. It constitutes one of the most powerful arguments against the policy of economic nationalism and autarky. At the same time, it serves as a guide to the entrepreneur in his attempt to obtain from his efforts and his venture the greatest possible profit and, concomitantly, to increase the supply in the market for the benefit of the consumer.

The *law of marginal utility* was formulated almost simultaneously by three economists of the last third of the nineteenth century: Carl Menger, Stanley Jevons, and Léon Walras. Until then economists had been perplexed by the paradox which resulted from the fact that, although iron is unquestionably more *necessary* and more *useful* than gold, the latter is nevertheless more highly esteemed, greater value is attached to it, and it commands a higher price in the market. The economists who formulated the theory of marginal utility took account of the fact that economic utility is the power to satisfy any want, even though the latter may be altogether capricious, like the vanity of wearing jewelry. Hence, the difference between the utility of iron and that of gold is not determined by comparing the serviceability of *all* the gold and *all* the iron in the world, but consists in the difference between the economic services, expressed in terms of supply and demand, that can be rendered by the *last available unit* of the one or the other metal. Consequently, even though an iron or a steel building is objectively more useful than a gold wristwatch, since iron is much more abundant than gold, it is natural that the last available unit of gold in the market should be economically much more useful and in demand, and therefore much more costly in terms of money, than the last unit of iron.

The theory of marginal utility demonstrates, in effect, that the economic measure of the utility of a thing is a function of its scarcity in relation to the needs of the market. Though advertising may sometimes succeed in creating in the consumers a need for certain things, the entrepreneur must still take into account, in calculating the probability of success in the market, the concept of the utility of his product in terms of public demand rather than his own ideas of its usefulness. It makes no sense to go to the market to offer chewing gum to those who want to buy tobacco, however innocuous the former may be and however harmful the latter. The truth of this law and the relativity involved in its application are confirmed by what happened during the first World War. In the middle of the war Germany found itself short of many things, among them iron, the supply of which was almost completely exhausted, while coal was abundant. As its geographical and military situation enabled it to make imports, which it needed to pay for in gold, the government made an appeal to the patriotism of the German people, and they responded by giving up their gold jewels in exchange for garish iron imitations that carried engraved on them the phrase, "I have given gold for iron." Practically no gold was left in Germany in private hands. But there was also a great scarcity of iron and other metallic objects, especially kitchen utensils. People valued iron highly and preferred it to any gold jewel that could be offered to them. For several years in Germany the marginal utility of iron was much greater than that of gold.

The *law of diminishing returns,* more recently known simply as *the law of returns* or also as *the law of the proportionality of the factors of production,* was first formulated by economists in its application to land. They noted that the yield from a given piece of land could be increased by the application of labor and other means of production such as machines and fertilizers, but only up to a certain point. Beyond this the increased expenditure invested in its more intensive exploitation was not translated into a corresponding increase in production, but resulted simply in an increase in unit costs: the land no longer yielded more, but, in a certain sense, less, because the product became more costly once the point had been passed at which the land had yielded its *optimum return*. Hence one spoke of "diminishing returns."

Later it was observed that this law is applicable to any and every form of production. In a shoe factory, for example, the employment of more modern machinery, an increase in the number of workers, the utilization of more or better auxiliary materials, such as dyes, lubricants, etc., will result in an increase in the net return more or less in proportion to the means employed. But a time will come when the optimum return is obtained, and if one seeks to go beyond this point with a more lavish use of the means of production, the return, instead of rising, will fall. This is something that needs to be carefully taken into account by the entrepreneur in making his economic calculation. He will have to pay heed to the particular circumstances of time and place in which production is to be carried on (such as the kind of motive power that is available; the supply, the quality, and the price of industrial labor; the cost of auxiliary materials; etc.), and he must calculate or discover by experience the precise combination of all the factors of production that, in the given time and place, will produce the optimum yield. If he does not do this and allows himself to be dazzled by appearances, by the example of other countries or other times, etc., then he runs the risk of obtaining, instead of a greater, a lesser return on his investment, to his own detriment and that of the market.

Among the problems of economic calculation confronting the entrepreneur, that of time stands in the forefront. Indeed, one might go so far as to say that entrepreneurial activity consists essentially in *the struggle against time*.

The economy is not something static, knowledge of which, once acquired, holds good forever. It is, on the contrary, a living thing which undergoes continuous variations, and consequently the data of the market today are not what they were yesterday or what they will be tomorrow. The raw materials available, technical advances, and the way of life, the tastes, and the wants of the consumers are constantly changing. On the other hand, a very important role in the economic calculation of the entrepreneur is played by the *rhythm of production.* By this is understood not only production properly so called, but also the process of distribution involved in bringing a particular thing or service to the ultimate consumer, for until this point is reached, an investment of capital and labor still has to be made; only when a commodity reaches the market can its price be determined. Corresponding to the greater or lesser rapidity of this rhythm will be the greater or lesser amount of circulating capital needed by the entrepreneur; an error in the calculation of this amount can lead to the failure of the enterprise.

The entrepreneur has to foresee the rhythm of his *turnover* so that he can calculate and make provision for the amount of the circulating capital that the enterprise is going to need. At the same time, he must also calculate the quantity of immobile means of production that he needs, which will determine the amount of fixed capital to be invested in the business. But this foresight must likewise extend, so far as possible, into *the future configuration of the market:* he has, in a certain sense, to foretell whether and how long the production that he wishes to undertake will find a market, whether the demand for his product will increase or diminish, whether prices will rise or fall in the course of time. This will tell him how far he can or ought to *risk* the available capital, how rapidly he has to amortize fixed investments, and many other things determining the volume and character of his business.

It is easy to understand, then, that none of these many calculations, which in their totality constitute economic calculation, can be exact: all are *calculations of probabilities,* and, a fortiori, so is the total economic calculation.

Statistics, provided always that they are exact and rightly interpreted, *tell us only what has happened up to the present, not what will happen tomorrow.* Technological progress is not *{diternot}* always predictable: revolutionary inventions sometimes come like a bolt from the blue; political or international events occasionally destroy in an unforeseen and unforeseeable way all the hopes based on the availability and price of raw materials; and it is even more difficult to anticipate the reactions of the consumers to these events. Who would have expected, for example, that at the outbreak of the First World War, when a scarcity of textiles became evident, women would persist in their refusal to wear short, narrow skirts and demand long, wide ones? However many data the entrepreneur takes into account in undertaking or managing his business—commercial geography, history and statistics, books and periodicals on the latest technological advances and those continually in progress—his decisions will always come up against an unknown quantity that he will have to determine by *intuition* on his own responsibility and in the spirit of adventure: he knows what happened yesterday and today, but tomorrow is in the hands of Providence. In a word: *every enterprise,* every business, every economic act in general, because it occurs and develops in time as well as in space, is *necessarily a speculation that can result in profit, but can also result in loss.*

Production, around which all economic life revolves, is, then, the great adventure of mankind: it is the struggle with tomorrow, the struggle with the unknown. The champion, the hero, and frequently the victim in this struggle is the entrepreneur. He undertakes some enterprise in quest of profit. But in order to obtain it, he is obliged to satisfy the consumer, that is to say, the public in general. Competition takes care of this. The consumer never loses. The entrepreneur, on the other hand, can see all his hopes of profit transformed into a loss that he alone must bear: the profit that the consumers (the general public) made is theirs to keep, while the entrepreneur is ruined. *This is an unavoidable necessity.* We have already seen that it cannot be avoided by any scientific cognition because the future is an unknown quantity that eludes every calculation and all foresight.

But can all this be avoided by political means? We shall concern ourselves later with the proposals that have been advanced and even tried with this object in view, whether by way of a change in the whole economic system or by way of corrective measures designed to overcome the alleged "weaknesses of free enterprise." But here we can already anticipate this much: *What the entrepreneur cannot foresee, nobody can foresee,* because, as we have said, science is impotent in the face of the unknown. The only thing that the state can do is to extricate the individual entrepreneur from his loss by depriving him of his profit, that is to say, *to assume the risk of the entrepreneur,* or rather, to make the general public take the risk, because the state has no other resources than those it takes from the people. In this dilemma, it would appear to be more sensible for the entrepreneur to run the risk rather than the general public.

4

Capital, Labor, and Wages

Utility and disutility. Production as creative. Capital and profit. Labor and wages. The "wages-fund" theory. The "iron law of wages." The labor theory of value. "Social injustice."

The essence of the market could be aptly described by saying that *it consists in obtaining utilities in exchange for disutilities.*

Utilities can be either goods or services, although the former almost always to some extent comprise the latter, even if only by virtue of the fact that the commodities in question are placed at the disposal of the consumers. A disutility consists in the deprivation one experiences from the lack of something or in the pains one takes to render some service.

This exchange of utilities for disutilities occurs directly more often than one might think. The black market in time of peace in countries more or less socialist, and in all countries in time of war, is, in fact, the real market and almost always involves direct barter transactions, since the scarcity of goods and services under such conditions causes people to consider money as of little worth. Normally, however, this exchange is effected indirectly through the medium of money. One does not engage in barter; one buys or sells. But this in no way alters the essential character of the market, because whoever pays money for a commodity has first obtained the cash in exchange for some disutility, by the expenditure of some kind of effort, and whoever sells a

29

commodity for money can use the cash thus obtained to buy
something that, for its purchaser, will be a utility and, for its
seller, a disutility.

The disutility in exchange for which a utility (i.e., a commodity) is obtained in the market is what is called *production*.
This is the physical and mental exertion needed to place a
commodity at the disposal of the consumer. In this sense we
are all producers, just as we are all consumers. Producer and
consumer are not members of two distinct social classes; production and consumption are rather two functions that everyone
performs every day without even realizing it. However, in the
strictly economic sense, a producer is anyone in the business of
supplying the market with utilities. A producer is thus not only
one who cultivates the soil or manufactures machines or consumers' goods, but anyone who is engaged in placing utilities
within reach of the consumer, for him to take or to leave. From
the economic point of view, things are not made or services
rendered; *utilities are produced*, since the ultimate stage in
the whole productive process is that at which these utilities become available to the purchaser.

Production signifies creation, though not, of course, in the
strict sense of the word. As Lavoisier said, nothing in this world
is either gained or lost; everything is simply transformed into
something else. But to transform iron into a machine or gold into
a jewel, or even to transform mere possibilities for travel into a
route available to the tourist on vacation, is, from the economic
point of view, an act of creation. Economically considered, creation is the realization of an idea, the accomplishment of a purpose. A *producer, then, is one who, in a general way, converts
possibilities into actualities by setting himself a goal and then
employing the means to attain it. The sole producer, in this sense,
is the *entrepreneur*. It is a mistake to refer to capitalists, technicians, and workers as *productive forces*. No one but the entrepreneur is a producer; the rest simply provide the services and
materials of which he avails himself in carrying on the process
of production.

The means of which the entrepreneur makes use are *capital* and *labor*. Capital consists of all the material factors that the entrepreneur employs to keep production in progress, from the land, buildings, machinery, and equipment, to the cash needed to maintain the cycle of production through reinvestment of the proceeds. It thus includes money as well as things, though the latter too are expressed in monetary terms in the calculations of the entrepreneur. The capital invested in an enterprise can be the property of the individual entrepreneur, or it can be provided by a number of people: one or more active entrepreneurs, either on their own or in association with capitalists who exercise no initiative in the conduct of the enterprise but share in its risks. From the economic point of view, all of them are entrepreneurs because they all assume the risk. In such cases, they generally form an association with a juridical personality, which constitutes the enterprise. Since, as we have seen, *capital goods* can consist of things whose value is expressible in monetary terms, and since the owners of these capital goods run a risk, we can define *capital* as *the money risked in an enterprise.*

What is the specific compensation received for the use of capital goods? It has been held by some to be rent and by others to be interest. Both opinions are erroneous and involve the possibility of confusion. Economics employs the term "rent" for something else entirely. Interest too is an altogether different thing from what it is generally believed to be. *The specific remuneration of capital is profit* and is characterized by the fact that it is essentially uncertain and aleatory. The capitalist runs the risk involved in the enterprise; he can make a profit or suffer losses. *Profit is justified, then, by the risk incurred.*

The other factor of production is *labor.* This is a disutility that one takes upon oneself in exchange for a utility, viz., wages. "Cursed is the ground for thy sake; in sorrow shalt thou eat of it all the days of thy life; in the sweat of thy face shalt thou eat bread," God says to Adam.[1] To be sure, throughout the ages labor has had its panegyrists, from the ancient Romans, who spoke of it as the foremost of the virtues *(labor prima virtus)*, to our own contemporaries, who have paid tribute to the "dignity" and the "joy" of labor and extolled "creative" work. Nevertheless, in the economic sense, *what is done purely for pleasure is not labor*— e.g., the work of the amateur artist or even that of the genius who feels himself called to a destiny to which he sacrifices everything; for neither of these activities is a means to an end; each is rather an end in itself. Labor is solely the more or less onerous exertion undertaken in exchange for the satisfaction of wants and desires and as a means of attaining this end.

A utility for the entrepreneur, labor is performed in exchange for wages, which represent for the worker utilities that he considers as more valuable than the effort he expends in return for them: the support of his family, the preservation of good health, opportunities for education and, as far as possible, recreation, and the possibility of periodic vacations and retirement in old age.

It has been said that labor is not a commodity, but in the economic domain this is not true at all. What is not a commodity is the worker, any more than is the entrepreneur or the capitalist. But labor, considered as a service, is a commodity, just like the services provided by the entrepreneur. *Everything that has a price in the market is a commodity* and, as such, is subject to the law of supply and demand.

 In the so-called labor market, as in every market, each party seeks to receive more than he gives. The boss gives for the labor of the worker an amount that he considers less than the service he is getting in exchange; the worker, for his part, renders a service that he considers as less valuable than his wage. And the same holds true of the entrepreneur when he renders on behalf of the enterprise services that go beyond those concerned with minimizing his own risks, viz., when he performs some technical task or seeks to reduce the risks of his associates. For this kind of service he receives from the enterprise a remuneration that for him is worth more, and for his associates less, than the effort he puts forth. If he asks too much, the capitalists turn him down and seek some other, less expensive technician; if they offer him too little, it is he who goes in search of other capitalists. His situation in this respect is no different from that of any day laborer.

In the spirit of the classical school, an attempt has been made to find objective laws that would determine wages independently of the will of the parties concerned. The oldest is the so-called *wages-fund theory*, which was developed principally by Price, Smith, McCulloch, Mill, and Fawcett. According to this theory, the height of wages is determined automatically in an economic community (what is meant is the economy of a country) by the portion of capital that the entrepreneurs can devote to wages (the wages fund) and by the number of workers who are to share in it. If prosperity permits the entrepreneurs to augment the wages fund, each worker gets an increase in pay. If the opposite occurs, or if the number of workers becomes greater as a consequence of an increase in the population, the pay of each worker is correspondingly reduced. If a group of workers succeeds in some way in winning a wage increase, this can only be at the expense of the rest of their comrades in the working class.

This theory, whose defects we shall consider later, was revived in a different form at the end of the last century by Böhm-Bawerk and Taussig. According to them, we should be concerned, not with nominal or money wage rates, but with real wages, i.e., with the goods that the worker can buy with the money in his pay envelope. The existing supply of goods in a country is limited. This stock of goods has to be divided among such uses as the maintenance and improvement of the material factors of production, so that it can be kept in progress and even expanded; the maintenance of the personnel and materials needed for public services, from the post office to the army, paid for out of taxes; and, finally, the support of the participants in the process of production, from the entrepreneur to the worker. There is no point in raising money wages if the goods themselves do not increase proportionately, because then prices will rise and in the end the worker will be able to purchase no more with his new salary than he could with the old.

Prior in origin, but more recent in its formulation, is the doctrine of the *iron law of wages*. This was early suggested by the physiocrats Turgot and Necker and later given definitive form by Ferdinand Lassalle (1825–1864), the founder of the German workers' movement, at that time to some extent allied with Marx; the influence of his ideas was still considerable in the German Social Democratic party before the Second World War (e.g., in the famous Erfurt program) and even in the Second International. According to this doctrine, the average wage always tends to be reduced to the minimum amount of indispensable necessities of life required to maintain and replace the labor force at the level of bare physiological subsistence. It cannot be raised much above this without resulting in an excessive birth rate among the working population, whose increased pressure on the labor market would then depress wages. It cannot, on the other hand, fall far below the subsistence minimum without adversely affecting the birth rate among the workers and giving rise to emigration, a reduction in their numbers, and a scarcity of labor.

Karl Marx founded his doctrine of wages on his theory of value. The value of a commodity depends on the amount of labor required to produce it. The labor of a skilled worker represents a multiple of that of an unskilled hired hand. In like manner, the value of the worker is measured by the cost of supporting him and of rearing and training a replacement with precisely the degree of skill needed; and the training, maintenance, and replacement of a skilled worker costs a multiple of the amount needed for the same purposes in the case of an ordinary unskilled laborer. This is what determines the price of labor in the market, i.e., wages. But the cost of supporting a worker is always less than what his labor produces. This difference is the *surplus value* which the entrepreneur retains, thereby depriving the worker of *the full proceeds of his labor.*

In criticism of these doctrines, the first point to be noted is that they are not scientific explanations of the way in which the mechanism of wages actually functions in the economy, but political lucubrations that are supposed to explain why the lower classes live in penury and to constitute a basis for a program of social reform. Even before Marx, Adam Smith, the founder of the classical school—which has been gratuitously accused of seeking to defend egoism and to justify servitude to those whom fortune has favored—had devoted a part of his famous book to a moving description of the sufferings of the poor, castigating the evils of the economic system of his age and proposing a number of reforms designed to redress what is today called *social injustice*.

All this is perfectly natural and even laudable. Neither economics nor anything else is studied solely out of pure curiosity to know the truth for its own sake, but in order to provide a sound basis for appropriate action. On the other hand, nothing is more commendable than to devote oneself to improving the lot of one's fellow men. But, in the first place, it is not scientific to confound matters of fact with wishes and desires, and even less to distort the facts in order to justify one's desires, however noble the latter may be. In the second place, there is no doubt that any schemes for reform that are based on erroneous beliefs about matters of fact are doomed to failure. An ostrichlike policy can lead to nothing but disaster. One has to look the facts boldly in the face. Only the truth can serve as a basis for successful action. This is what makes modern critical economics a science. It does not give advice; it is concerned purely and exclusively with matters of fact brought to light by honest investigation and rendered coherent by reflection. And, as regards wages, the facts are, essentially, as follows:

1. It is not accurate to say that wages depend on economic conditions in a particular community or country. They ultimately depend on international competition. This determines the prices of raw materials and manufactured products on the world market, from which no nation can withdraw if it does not want to be eliminated in this competition; and, by the same token, the latter determines the margin that remains, after other expenses have been paid, for the compensation of the entrepreneur and the

worker. It even directly determines the height of wages because, other things being equal, the worker always goes where he can get the best pay.

2. It is not true that in every country the total amount of wages is determined by the fund that production can make available for that purpose or by the existing supply of consumers' goods or by the minimum generally needed by the worker for his bare subsistence and replacement as such, and that this amount is then equally divided among the workers. Even in countries in which minimum wages are fixed by law, each branch of production, as well as each enterprise within it, has its own rate of wages determined, on the one hand, by the margin left over by competition from the prices of its products, and, on the other hand, by the greater or lesser and more or less organized supply of available labor. Nor are the workers in any particular branch of production content, for their part, to accept as payment for their services an amount determined solely by the fact that it is the prevailing rate of wages in other branches of production. On the contrary: they struggle to obtain higher wages if this is at all possible as a result of the scarcity of labor in their own branch or through the power of their trade-union; and even then the especially skillful or productive worker, who considers his labor as having a greater utility, demands a correspondingly higher wage than his comrades, and, if he does not get it, withholds his labor and offers it to another entrepreneur who better appreciates its value.

3. Nor is it precisely correct to say that wages are paid from the capital of the entrepreneur; they are ultimately paid by the consumer, for they constitute one of the elements that enter into the formation of the sales price. But even if this were not so, the wages-fund doctrine does not provide any criterion for determining how the wages fund is established.

4. Equally worthless as a criterion is the minimum indispensable for the nurture and subsistence of the worker. There is no objective standard for determining this amount. The worker of the present day, if he avoids ostentatious extravagance or intemperate self-indulgence, lives much better than Croesus in all

his opulence or Louis XIV in all his splendor; and yet he complains of living poorly, and we agree with him. According to statistics, and taking into account fluctuations in the value of money, the real wages and standard of living of the French worker have doubled since 1848, and those of the American worker have quintupled; but as their material and cultural needs have likewise increased, their wages continue to represent, psychologically, a subsistence minimum. That it is practically impossible to state precisely what this minimum is may be seen from the fact that of two workers of equal competence and with the same family obligations and the same wages, one lives well and is able to save, while the other lives poorly and finds his pay inadequate.

5. It is not true that the value of commodities is measured by the quantity of labor they contain, or that the value of a worker is measured by the cost of his nurture, sustenance, and replacement by a worker in the same category. The first of these doctrines has already been refuted; and in regard to the second, it must be objected that when an entrepreneur hires a worker, he takes into account neither the cost of the latter's nurture and training nor that of his present necessities as a qualified worker nor the ease or difficulty with which the worker may be able to rear and educate his own offspring as he himself was educated. The sole consideration in hiring a worker is his fitness for the job and the price of his labor. A good proof of this is provided by those so-called "white-collar proletarians" who receive salaries that neither compensate for what they cost their parents nor make it possible for their own children to receive the same education that they did.

6. The fact is that wages are determined by supply and demand, and not in a general way, but in each case, by branches of production, by enterprises within each one of these branches, and by individuals within each enterprise, on the basis of the existing need for labor, its abundance or scarcity, and the productive capability of each particular worker. This holds true not only in countries with a system of free enterprise but also in those with a more or less interventionist policy, like Mexico,

and even in countries with a socialist economy, like Russia, where, as Davies notes,[2] the differences in wages among the various branches of production and among individuals within each one of them are much greater than they are in the United States. This is evidenced by Stakhanovism and by the intelligentsia, a class of scientists, artists, and political functionaries that enjoys the greatest abundance amidst the general penury.

Up to now no better method of determining wage rates has been found than that of the market. The attempts to give *to each according to his needs* and to demand *from each according to his abilities* have failed every time they have been made (as they were in Russia at the beginning of the Bolshevik Revolution), for the simple reason that everything that the worker earns in wages, beyond what he would receive through the unhampered operation of the mechanism of supply and demand, he has to pay out in his capacity as a consumer because of the increase in prices thereby brought about. Nor is it possible, as we shall see later, to raise wages at the expense of entrepreneurial profits.

7. From what has already been said, it also follows that it is absurd to attempt *to give the worker a share in the management and the profits.* Profits are the compensation of the entrepreneur for the risk he assumes. For him to be able to take the risk exclusively on his own account, he requires all the independence correlative with his responsibility. The worker assumes neither the risk nor the responsibility of the enterprise and therefore has no claim to participation either in its management or in its profits. One can speculate about the possibility of an economy without entrepreneurial risk. But the workers' participation in the management and profits of the enterprise is a hybrid and, as such, sterile solution of the problem.

5

Money and Credit

Direct and indirect exchange. Barter and money. The history of money. Monetary theories. The money market. Credit and interest. Inflation and deflation. The price of money. Stable money. The gold standard.

At least since the time of Xenophon attempts have been made to formulate a completely integrated and coherent theory of money that would provide a comprehensive explanation of its value and its fluctuations. But what renders this difficult, not to say impossible, is not only the twofold function of money as both a medium of exchange and a commodity with a value of its own but also the interference of psychological and political factors in monetary affairs. Economists have been able to ascertain the causes of the value of money in relation to other monetary systems or to other things and services, but they have not been able to discover and are hardly likely to discover any single formula that can explain all these phenomena.

Logically and doubtless also historically, the originary form of the market and of the division of labor is barter. Direct exchange is converted into indirect exchange when the owner of something perishable or having but an intermittent or sporadic utility seeks to trade it directly for something more durable and more likely to be a regular item of consumption (salt, wheat, oil, cotton, etc.), in order to obtain with it, at an opportune time, other things or services that he may need. The commodity that is procured in the first of these transactions acquires the character of a *medium of exchange*. This medium of exchange is then perfected in the form of *money*.

Originally anything that was simply rare—and whose acquisition therefore involved a certain amount of labor on the part of whoever obtained it directly from Nature—like the shells of certain molluscs or the eyeteeth of certain animals, served as money. Later precious metals were used for this purpose, having a utility in themselves as well as in their capacity as media of exchange. Since it was both difficult and dangerous to lay up a great store of these metals, they were entrusted in the Middle Ages to goldsmiths, who issued receipts for the amount left with them on deposit. These receipts would then pass from hand to hand as their holders used them in payment for goods and services. Hence arose the business of banking. Instead of giving receipts for the sums placed on deposit with them, the bankers issued bank notes whose bearers could convert them into metallic money at the bank of issue, which backed them with the deposits.

In this way money accumulates in banks, and as depositors do not normally need to have all their money at their immediate disposal, banks pay them *interest* (with certain exceptions), the amount being smaller in the case of *demand* deposits, which can be withdrawn by the depositor at any time without prior notice, and larger in the case of *time* deposits, which are not payable before a definite date. Keeping on hand only what is needed to provide for anticipated withdrawals, the banks *lend* the surplus, charging the borrowers a higher rate of interest in order to earn a profit and cover their risk, and extend *credit* to those who merit their confidence or pledge a certain amount as security. Thus, *bank accounts* and *checks*, which are given and accepted in lieu of money, make their appearance.

And it is at this point that two kinds of governmental interference thenceforth take place. First, in order to prevent fraud in regard to the quality and the quantity of the precious metals serving as money, the practice of *assaying* and *monetizing* them is established, whereby they are certified as to weight and purity, stamped into *coins* of various denominations having a *face value* fixed by law (so many mills of fine metal for every one thousand of the alloy), and carefully *minted*. Then the government proceeds to establish a control over the banks in order to prevent them from issuing more *fiduciary media* (i.e., money-substitutes) than they have in cash on deposit. This control is entrusted to the *central bank*, to which the government grants a monopoly over the issuance of bank notes *redeemable* in metallic money. More recently, these bank notes have been rendered irredeemable and declared *legal tender*, and the central banks have been authorized to issue more notes than correspond to their *reserves* of precious metal or *cash holdings*. Then too, many countries have established an *embargo* on gold and silver and have withdrawn them from circulation, reserving them solely for the use of the government or of the central bank, except in amounts destined for nonmonetary uses. The final step is taken when the government is free to determine, more or less under the control of the legislative power, the amount of *fiat money* in circulation, i.e., paper money that is backed by nothing more in the way of reserves or security (even though an attempt may be made to hold in the central bank the greatest possible amount of specie or of foreign exchange in good repute) than the credit of the government or the confidence of the people in its fiscal and monetary policy.

This, briefly, has been the sad history of money—a history that has not been lacking in miracle-workers who profess to see in it happy auguries full of promise.

Let us now turn our attention to the *theories of money*. These, in the order in which they have appeared historically, can be reduced to three: the *quantity* theory, the *qualitative* theory, and the theory of the *neutrality of money*.

The quantity theory of money was first formulated by Jean Bodin, a Frenchman (also known as Bodinus, 1520–1596), whom many regard as the founder of scientific economics. Impressed, no doubt, by the enormous rise in prices in sixteenth-century Spain consequent upon the importation of precious metals from the New World, Bodin held that the value of money in a country is inversely proportional to the supply of goods on the market: the more money and the fewer goods, the less value (i.e., *purchasing power*) money has, and vice versa. The core of truth in this doctrine is the fact that money is a medium of exchange and, in relation to the goods and services that can be bought or sold, is subject to the law of supply and demand. Even today this theory cannot be entirely rejected, but it suffers from two defects:

1. It is based on the assumption of an autarkic economy, i.e., that the money in question circulates only in one country and can purchase only the commodities for sale in that country; whereas in fact money, as well as commodities, has an international circulation, so that a country with an abundant supply of money and a scarcity of goods can be a rich country if outside its borders there is a scarcity of money and an abundance of goods.

2. It is based, morever, on the assumption that money is nothing but a medium of exchange, and that its only role in the market is as a means of payment for goods and services. But money, as we shall see, has other functions besides, which give it, as it were, a life of its own, and which appreciably influence its value according to the supply of and the demand for it.

The qualitative theory, which appears to have been formulated by John Locke (1632–1704), holds that the value of money is the intrinsic value of the metal it contains or represents. In this theory as well there is a core of truth that cannot be disregarded today, but it too fails to give an exhaustive explanation of the causal factors that determine the value of money. According to it, the Mexican peso, with the modest gold reserves in the Bank of Mexico, should be worth much less than what it is worth today, and, on the other hand, the dollar, with fifty per cent of the world's gold in Fort Knox, should be worth much more.*

The theory of the neutrality of money, attributed to another great Englishman, David Hume (1711–1776), was later held by

* [The reader is reminded that the original Spanish-language edition of this book was published in 1956.—TRANSLATOR.]

John Stuart Mill and has since been accepted by many other economists up to the present day. According to them, money is merely a *token* of the value of things, or a means of calculating their value, without there being any reciprocal influence between money, on the one hand, and goods and services, on the other.

This doctrine goes astray because it is founded on a purely theoretical and provisional assumption, to which economics has recourse solely as an heuristic device to facilitate the study of the phenomena of the market, namely, that all exchange is essentially barter. But this methodological postulate, framed merely as a means of rendering an understanding of the market easier by isolating it, for specific purposes, from all other economic phenomena, in no way corresponds to what actually takes place. In the real world, there is interposed, between the goods exchanged on the market, another commodity, viz., money. Things are not exchanged for things, but for money, and the relation between every commodity and money is subject to the law of supply and demand: a thing is dear or cheap according as it costs more or less money. There is thus a fundamental difference between barter and the market properly so called. Barter is direct and bilateral, whereas the market, as expressed in money prices, is indirect and multilateral. Hence, it follows that money, as a commodity that is exchanged for things, has a value of its own that is determined by market factors, and in particular by its better or poorer quality and by its abundance or scarcity. More or fewer goods are sold for money according to the value attributed to it. One money is preferred to another. It is valued more highly if it is scarce and less highly if it is abundant. This does not mean that it therefore ceases to be a token of payment, but it is not only that; it is also a commodity in its own right, with a utility derived from its material and its function and a price determined by the demand for it and the supply of it.

Thus, none of the three theories of money that we have summarized is adequate in itself; all three must be taken together. Each one of them explains only a part of the truth, and perhaps something still remains to be explained. In any case, money is a medium and a token of exchange, as the theory of its neutrality asserts. It also has an intrinsic value as money by virtue of its material content as well as its specific utility, e.g., in making hoarding possible, as the qualitative theory holds. And, as the quantity theory recognizes, the purchasing power of money stands in a more or less mathematical relation to the supply of and the demand for goods on the market.

This brings us to the concept of the *money market,* about which there likewise prevails a good deal of confusion. People speak of money as abundant or scarce, as cheap or dear, without making any distinction between *money* and *credit,* although the two are altogether different from each other in their mechanism.

When businessmen speak of money as scarce or abundant, as "tight" or "easy," they are not, in fact, referring to money at all, but to credit, especially bank credit, or the loan market. Thus, not long ago it was reported that the Bank of England had raised the *discount rate* on short-term (i.e., ninety-day) loans. This brought about an increase in the *price of money*—i.e., the *rate of interest*—another matter about which a fundamental error has prevailed since even before the days of the classical economists.

It is commonly said that "money begets money." Indeed, some economists have gone so far as to assert that interest is the specific product of money, and that a loan is the *renting of money.* He who needs money hires it; that is to say, he borrows it and pays the lender, by way of rent, if not all, then a part of the product that the money will yield him. But the fact is that money is sterile. What is productive is labor in the broadest sense of the word: the labor of the entrepreneur, aided by the other factors and means of production. One of these is circulating capital. Now it sometimes happens that there is a scarcity of capital, so that the entrepreneur has to wait for a longer period for the final proceeds. He could then buy, with the money obtained from the sale of the product—a sum that he has not so far been able to get—raw materials enabling him to produce and sell more. With more money he could buy more machines and factors of production and expand his business. Now he has to wait. If he can find the money, he can have today what otherwise he must wait for until tomorrow. Thus, when he obtains a loan, he does not hire money; *he hires time.* The interest that he pays is the price of the advantage that he gains in having today what otherwise he would not have until tomorrow.

The value of a present good is always greater than that of a future good. For this reason the most common form of commercial loan is the *discount.* When the holder of a bill of exchange collectible in ninety days presents it for discount at the bank, he is advanced the amount of its face value less a deduction based on the discount rate, i.e., the prevailing rate of interest. The businessman pays this interest if it is worth less to him than the advantage of having immediately available the remaining amount of the face value of the bill in order to be able to employ the cash for the purchase of means of production. The same holds true for whoever lends money, whether a bank or a private individual, over the long or the short term. It is an advantage to have cash on hand. With this money one can, at any given moment, buy something that one wants or avail oneself of a good business opportunity that may arise in the future; or even in normal, peaceful times one can hope that prices may fall and one's money may be worth more. But in the meanwhile the money is idle and produces no income. If someone offers for its use, by way of interest, an amount that seems to the owner of the money to be worth more than the aforementioned advantages of hoarding it, he will put it out on loan, because he prefers the immediate gain to the future gain. He too *discounts time.*

What, then, gives rise to the *rate of interest,* or the price of money? Nothing more nor less than the supply of it and the demand for it. Whoever has cash on hand demands, in exchange for the loan of it, a rate of interest that will yield him a greater advantage than he expects to gain by keeping the money. Whoever borrows money offers for it, by way of interest, an amount that he finds it less burdensome to pay than to wait until he obtains his own money. The outcome of the co-ordination of these mutual desires is the rate of interest.

What we have just described is the mechanism in the individual case. However, as there is not just one person who has money and one who needs it, but many who have it and many who would like to have it, and since nobody will lend money to anybody else at a rate of interest lower than what a third party is prepared to pay, and vice versa, the *market rate of interest* is determined in the same way as all other prices on the market. This is, in any case, the essence of the process, even though in actual practice other factors do play a role: some psychological, like the increase in the demand for money during a boom, when producers wish to take advantage of all possibilities and are ready to pay a high rate of interest; others of an institutional nature, like the intervention of the government's central bank, which rediscounts the credit operations of private banks at a rate that to some extent affects their own discount rate.

All this refers to money loaned on credit, i.e., money considered as an auxiliary means of production and made available in what is called—according to whether the loan is for a short or a long term—the *money market* or the *capital market* (even though the two are not strictly the same; for money on loan, in spite of running a certain risk, does not run the specific risk of the capital of the entrepreneur or of the stockholder: it does not share in his gains or losses in direct proportion to the success or failure of the enterprise in which it is invested). But the primary function of money properly so called is to serve as a medium of exchange, and in that capacity it gives rise to other problems, such as its national and international *exchange rate*, its *purchasing power*, and the general influence it exercises on the market and on business by virtue of the phenomena of *inflation* and *deflation*. These problems have such a close bearing on *economic*—and especially monetary—*policy* that we shall reserve their detailed investigation for a later chapter, limiting ourselves here to but a brief explanation.

As we have seen, it is through the medium of money that goods and services are exchanged in the market. As the supply of commodities in the market is limited, the quantity theory of money is, on the whole, correct in holding that if the quantity of money in the hands of purchasers increases or decreases, they will be able to buy, with the same money, a lesser or a greater quantity of goods and services. The quotient represented by the total supply of available commodities divided by the total quantity of available money is, other things being equal, the *purchasing power* of the latter. An increase in the supply of money without any corresponding increase in the supply of commodities is called *inflation;* the contrary phenomenon is called *deflation.* Inflation occurs whenever the exploitation of gold mines results in an increase in the quantity of money relatively to the total supply of goods and services; and deflation occurs whenever there is an increase in the population, and technical progress produces an abundance of commodities without any corresponding increase in the quantity of money in circulation.

There is a widespread belief that inflation is bad and that deflation is good, because the former diminishes the purchasing power of the consumers and makes foreign products more expensive, whereas deflation has the contrary effect. However, this mode of reasoning is not correct, because for the economy as a whole it makes no difference whether imported or domestic products cost more if more money is available and less if the opposite is the case. The *national economy* (if we may, for the moment, provisionally assume its existence) neither gains nor loses by inflation or deflation. In the long run the entire population consumes what it produces, either directly or by way of imports purchased with the foreign exchange made available by its exports and with other income from abroad, as from tourism, freightage for the cargoes transported by the national merchant marine, the proceeds from foreign investments, etc. As long as inflation and deflation occur in the normal course of events, their effects are produced slowly, their extent is small in comparison with the total amount of international trade, and the necessary adaptations can be made quite easily. But when they are abnormally produced—that is to say, when they are produced by the intervention of the government—they have mischievous consequences, for they *take from some in order to give to others.*

It is to these phenomena of government intervention that people are really referring, albeit unwittingly, when they inveigh against the evils of inflation in particular. Our present-day inflation is of this kind. It is produced when the government, in need of money, has recourse to the printing press. It costs the government no more to issue paper money than the expense of printing it. Yet this cheap money, now at the disposal of the government, is placed on a par with what the citizens have earned with their own labor. The supply of available commodities, not having increased concomitantly with the products of the government's printing presses, now has to be divided between the old money and the new. The whole process is very much like diluting wine with water. The government pours water into its citizens' wine and then appropriates a share of the watered wine for itself. With this it pays its expenses: the salaries of more or less unnecessary bureaucrats, the cost of machinery and materials for more or less unnecessary public works, and frequently the costs of wars that it has not succeeded in avoiding. All these payments are made in reality with the share of the good wine that the government has taken from its citizens by the process of pouring water into it, leaving each citizen with the same quantity of "wine," but of thinner consistency, and keeping the rest for itself. The whole procedure is hardly a whit better, morally, than clandestinely tapping an electric cable to draw off a part of the current for oneself without having it recorded on the meter and being obliged to pay for it. By such means governments arbitrarily dispose of the fruits of their citizens' laborious efforts to lay by a reserve for their old age and then redistribute the proceeds "for the benefit of the underprivileged." In fact, however, it is precisely the poor who are harmed the most by such a policy, in the first place because depriving a millionaire of thirty per cent of his possessions is not the same as taking a like amount from a worker or an employee of modest means, and in the second place because the upward adjustments in wages that are made in the course of an inflation never keep pace with the rise in prices and the cost of living. Otherwise, the government would not gain any advantage from the inflation.

It has been said in defense of inflation that it is beneficial to debtors because it permits them to pay off with money of inferior quality debts contracted in terms of good money. But the belief that all debtors are poor and all creditors are rich is a myth. Both rich and poor are to be found in each of these classes, and, in fact, it seems more likely that most debtors are rich, because nobody lends money to a person who is insolvent. It is always people of substance that are granted bank credit. On the other hand, their creditors, at least indirectly, are the banks' shareholders and the depositors, who are drawn from the great mass of people with small savings.

It is also an obvious error to say that deflation (or, in this case, the withdrawal of money from circulation by an act of government intervention) counteracts the bad effects of inflation by causing prices to decline. We have already stated that, for the economy as a whole, this is of no importance. What happens in the individual case is the following: During the course of the inflation debtors pay in bad money the amounts they have received in good money. If new debts are then contracted, payable in bad money, and if deflation ensues, they have to be paid in good money. Thus, the new debtors have to pay for the sins of the old. One injustice is heaped upon another.

For this reason some have advocated *stable money* as the ideal medium of exchange. However, the realization of this ideal is impossible, because, like every other commodity, *money is essentially unstable*. Even aside from government intervention, there are many unpredictable factors that influence its value. It is desirable, nevertheless, that money be as stable as possible, or, at least, that its fluctuations be kept within moderate bounds so that their repercussions may not be too sudden or severe. But how is this to be accomplished? People talk of keeping the money in circulation proportional to the volume or circulation of goods. But no one has succeeded in finding the formula of this equilibrium or the means of applying it. Such a policy requires a constantly flexible regulatory action that cannot be effected by laws or controlled by the power of the legislature, whose members neither have sufficient knowledge nor are able to stay in session day and night throughout the year. There is no other alternative than to give plenary powers to the executive and to charge him with the responsibility of regulating the supply of money with the aid of his technical advisers. This is what the executive authorities of most of the countries in the world say must be done today, and the unhappy results of such a policy are everywhere to be seen. It was not without reason that Lord Acton said, "All power corrupts, and absolute power corrupts absolutely."

This explains why people who have begun to see these matters in a clear light have turned anew to the idea of metallic money and are asking that gold come out of the depositories and vaults of the central banks and return to the pockets and purses of private individuals, for gold is the only really *sound money with intrinsic value*. The desire for a return to gold is understandable, and we hope to see it realized some day, although the argument in favor of the gold standard is not always stated in a valid way. The distinctive function of gold money does not consist in its intrinsic value or in the constancy of that value, which fluctuates even in the absence of government intervention. The excellence of metallic money in free circulation consists in the fact that it renders impossible the abuse of the power of the government to dispose of the possessions of its citizens by means of its monetary policy and thus serves as the solid foundation of economic liberty within each country and of free trade between one country and another.

6

Monopoly, Crises, and Unemployment

Monopoly and the French Revolution. Monopoly as a political phenomenon. Business-cycle theories. Boom and depression. Easy money. Unemployment in the modern world. Theories of unemployment. Keynes. Depression and unemployment.

The scientific study of economic phenomena began contemporaneously with the emergence of our modern industrial economy, and the subsequent development of economics has paralleled technological improvements in production as well as progress in such auxiliary fields as communications and banking. The economic theory with which we are familiar today is no less an offspring of the Industrial Revolution than is our actual economic system, which, rightly or wrongly, has been dubbed *capitalism.*

Among the phenomena that economists encountered in carrying on their investigations were monopolies, crises, and unemployment. They consequently took it for granted that these abnormalities are inherent characteristics of the capitalist system, or the economy of free enterprise. It is therefore appropriate to devote some attention to the nature of these three phenomena in order to see whether they are, in fact, compatible with modern capitalism, and whether they are produced by it or by other causes.

The word "monopoly" (from the Greek *monos* = only, and *polein* = to sell) means literally "one and only seller." Exclusive control can be exercised over a work of art, an invention, a whole class of commodities, or the supply of labor in a particular enterprise (as happens when labor unions bar from employment in it, by means of a "closed shop" contract, anyone outside their own ranks). In economics the term "monopoly" is used to denote any situation that interferes with the free play of supply and demand. Generally, however, what one has in mind in using the term is only a monopoly on the side of the suppliers of commodities in the market. One speaks of a tobacco monopoly, a match monopoly, a gasoline monopoly, a meat monopoly, etc., meaning that a person or a group of persons—or the government itself— has complete control over the supply of these commodities or at least a control sufficiently great to enable the monopolist to impose his prices on the public and to regulate consumption accordingly, limiting it to the quantity that he deigns to make available on the market.

Monopoly is as old as history. Already in the most ancient communities we find state monopolies of salt, of precious metals, of perfumes and dyes, and even, during the decline of the Roman Empire, of articles of prime necessity like cloth and cereals.

During the Middle Ages the guilds enjoyed a double monopoly: they controlled production, and they monopolized the labor force in each enterprise. The law granted the masters of the guilds the exclusive right to carry on production, to admit or reject new members, to educate the apprentices, and to train them to become masters. This situation continued into the era of the absolute monarchs, although the latter gradually arrogated to themselves many of the powers previously enjoyed by the guilds and granted licenses for production that enabled the Crown to bring in revenue to the state and, at the same time, to support its favorites at court. One has only to recall the monopolies that Henry II of France granted to his mistress, Diane de Poitiers. Indeed, a good part of the nobility lived off the income from monopolies.

Nor was England free of them. In fact, it was on their account that the Declaration of Independence of the United States proclaimed the principle of freedom of labor, or the right to the "pursuit of happiness." Similarly, on September 14, 1791, the French Constituent Assembly, after reaffirming the Declaration of the Rights of Man originally formulated during the period from August to October in 1789, declared an end to "nobility, peers, distinctions among the estates of the realm, feudal rights, hereditary judgeships, the sale or inheritance of public offices, privileges and exemptions from the law common to all Frenchmen, wardenships, and guilds of artisans, craftsmen, or members of the same profession." Later it promulgated the Constitution of 1791, of which Article 16 stated that "every citizen has the right to enjoy in freedom his property and income and the fruit of his labor and industry," and Article 19 granted every person freedom to "engage in such business or to practice such profession, art, or craft as he shall find profitable." A regime of economic liberty was established, and monopolies were suppressed. And, to prevent these same citizens from restricting this liberty and obstructing the free play of supply and demand by means of combinations in restraint of trade, the penal codes forbade and still forbid "conspiracies to effect a change in the price of goods." [1]

Monopoly, then, is not compatible with our modern economy. Indeed, it is impossible in a system of free enterprise. To be sure, there will always be entrepreneurs who, not content with the profits to be derived from the supply and demand on the market, will band together (however many "antimonopoly laws" there may be on the statute books) to monopolize particular commodities or services in order to obtain exorbitant prices for them. But where there is free enterprise there will not be lacking another group of entrepreneurs, no less powerful than the first, prepared to lure away their customers with lower prices. Free competition will then reassert itself, and the two groups will engage in a "price war" until the prices obtained leave only a normal profit. This is possible, of course, only if neither of the competing groups enjoys an official protection that the other does not have and that renders the protected group superior to its rival in the market. This protection, in the form of licenses authorizing the establishment of particular industries, prohibitively high tariffs on foreign products, tax exemptions, production or export subsidies, etc., may be extended in view of some well- or ill-understood national interest, or because the country is in a state of war, or simply, as in the days of Louis XIV, in order to grant favors to the friends (who sometimes are also the partners) of the authorities. In all countries there are innumerable cases of this kind in which it is not always possible to determine whether the motive is a desire on the part of the government to protect a more or less well-understood national interest or to prepare for war, or whether what is involved is nothing more nor less than official corruption. *But it is impossible to find a single example of a monopoly that has ever existed without official protection.*

The term "crisis" denotes a maladjustment in economic life that gives rise to a general depression, but one not caused by external circumstances like natural catastrophes, epidemics, wars, or revolutionary inventions or discoveries. A free economy involves a certain automatism, so that any partial disturbance of it is corrected by the action of the forces at work. Thus, if a commodity is produced in excess of the demand for it, its price falls, and production of it is restricted until the demand once again increases and prices normalize themselves. If a commodity is in short supply, its price rises and attracts to the market new producers, who cause the price to fall to a normal level. But there are times when this self-corrective process does not seem to occur, and crises arise. Then economists seek an explanation and a remedy for them. Since the time of Sismondi (1773–1842) crises have been described as periodic infirmities to which a free economy is subject (cyclical crises) and as a result of the "anarchy of production." Karl Marx held both views at the same time, although it is evident that they are mutually contradictory, since an economy in which there are periodic phenomena that can be calculated and predicted can hardly be characterized as anarchic.

If, as we have said, a crisis is a maladjustment in economic life, there can be many different kinds of crises. Generally, however, when one speaks of a crisis, what is meant is a crisis due to a falling off of sales, a failure of the market to absorb the products that are brought to it. It is not surprising, therefore, that the economists of an earlier age explained this kind of crisis by attributing it to a lack of money. Yet it is obvious that this explanation is not satisfactory. In general, commodities are distributed in accordance with the supply of money available. If this is meager, commodity prices will be low, but no disturbance will be produced in the economy. Commodities will be worth less, but money will be worth more, and consequently everything that is brought to the market will be absorbed. This is the way Adam Smith and Jean-Baptiste Say explain the matter, and no one has succeeded in refuting them.

A variant of this doctrine is that of *overproduction*. It has been said that the crisis occurs when producers produce beyond the needs of the consumers, so that there is a glut on the market; for the consumers, even though they have the money to buy the commodities offered for sale, simply do not want them. In reply to this contention one need only observe that, up to the present day, there has never been a time when the world has produced enough for everybody. The great economic problem is that of scarcity, which still continues to exist to a frightful extent. Mankind still does not produce enough to provide for even the most pressing necessities. A general overproduction of commodities is a myth, and not an actual fact. At any given time and place there may be a surplus of particular goods, but not of all goods. In such cases the mechanism we have already described comes into play, and normal conditions are restored without any important disturbances in the economy, even though the readjustment may ruin particular producers who have erred in calculating their production or in forecasting market conditions. This is a case of *uneven production*, which a third theory of the crisis considers as its explanation. But the core of truth in this doctrine—i.e., the occurrence of such local and temporary surpluses in the production of particular commodities—does not explain the crisis as a phenomenon of general economic disturbance.

Rodbertus, Marx, Henry George, and economists of their persuasion, as well as some more recent authors who consider themselves liberals, like Carlos P. Carranza,[2] explain the crisis as a result of the *concentration of capital*. According to them (in spite of some minor variations in their doctrines), the producers accumulate and employ in increasing production the *ground rent* and the *surplus value* that they withhold from society or from the worker, thereby reducing the purchasing power of the masses. At the moment when this money is reinvested in the construction of new units of production (factories, workshops, granaries, etc.), wages are distributed to many workers, and there is a *boom* in the market as more money flows into it although the supply of goods has not yet increased, since the new units in the process of construction are still not producing. By the time they finally do so, there is an abundance of commodities on the market that cannot be absorbed, and a crisis ensues. This explanation is also mythical and erroneous, because it never happens that all producers reap profits, save, and invest at the same time. Even if this were true of each one of them, there would still be lacking the necessary synchronization that would alone explain the general crisis.

Approaching the problem of crises from another point of view, the *currency school,* which appeared in England in the second half of the nineteenth century, and the *Viennese school* conceive of the cause in monetary terms. As we have already observed, money, although essentially a medium of exchange, has other functions and effects that give it a life of its own. Any abnormalities arising—or rather, induced—in the value of money convert it from a regulator into a disturber of economic life. In a word, *crises arise, not from a lack, but from an excess, of money.*

This does not mean that crises are caused by inflation. As we have seen, inflation, when it takes place in the natural course of events, does not disturb the equilibrium of the market. What is economically detrimental is the discrimination that results from an inflationary policy on the part of the government. A distinction therefore has to be made between inflation per se and *credit expansion,* otherwise known as an *easy-money* (or *cheap-money*) policy. Inflation takes place in the natural course of events whenever the supply of money on the market increases more than that of goods. This occurred in Europe when gold was shipped there from the Indies, and in the world in general during the period of the "gold fever" that accompanied the discoveries of new deposits of ore in the United States and South Africa. But when governments resort to the printing press to produce the currency needed to pay for the services and materials of a swelling bureaucracy and more or less spectacular programs of public works, what occurs is both an *inflation,* because more money enters the market without a corresponding increase in the supply of goods, and, at the same time, an *expansion of credit,* because the public works stimulate the development and growth, above and beyond the normal needs of the country, of industries engaged in carrying out the government program and unable to subsist without it.

Credit expansion pure and simple takes places when, in an effort to force an increase in the country's production beyond the normal development of its economic life, a policy is adopted —by the government, of course—of accelerating production, or, as W. A. Lewis [3] calls it, mobilizing resources. This policy consists simply in making money available (generally in the form of bank credit at low interest rates) to those who wish to establish or expand branches of production that are considered advantageous to the country. A boom supervenes: factories or farmhouses are built; machinery is manufactured, imported, and set up; a bureaucratic personnel is organized. All this means money passing through many hands and reaching the market to buy consumers' goods that have not increased to the same extent. The result is that, in accordance with the law of supply and demand, and in spite of the price ceilings imposed by the government, prices rise. With the increase in prices, wages too have to be raised, and there is an illusion of prosperity. But a time comes when the

money available for the expansion of production is used up, and
the industries thus created have to live on their own resources.
Very few can do so. Some industries prove to have been poor
investments and go out of business entirely. Others produce goods
for which there is no demand, like machinery for still other
industries that have not expanded or consumers' goods that are
priced too high to compete with those already on the domestic
or foreign market. A crisis results: prices have risen, the value of
the monetary unit has depreciated, production useful and necessary to the country has not increased, sales fall off, workers
lose their jobs, unemployment is on the rise, and a painful
period of readjustment begins. The policy of credit expansion,
instead of increasing the wealth of the country, has dissipated
a good part of it. One is reminded of the old story of the milkmaid and the pitcher of milk. With the proceeds from the sale
of the milk she dreams of buying some sheep; from the sheep
she hopes to get enough to purchase a cow; etc., etc. But in the
midst of her daydreams the milkmaid stumbles, the pitcher is
shattered, and nothing remains but her tears. If one tries to
build on illusions, one is sure to suffer disillusionment sooner
or later.

We have seen, then, that crises, like monopolies, do not and
cannot have any place in an economy of free enterprise. They
are not essential elements or necessary effects of it; neither are
they defects in it. They are, on the contrary, the *consequences
of political interference with the free-market economy.*

As we shall see, the same holds true for unemployment.
As long as methods of production remained primitive, unemployment was unknown. The wretched poverty that prevailed
before the Industrial Revolution was due precisely to the meager
productivity of the methods then in use and to the lack of the
manpower needed to produce enough to satisfy the necessities of
everyone. The introduction of machinery, above all in the
English textile and weaving industry, left large numbers of
workers jobless. Much more yarn and many more fabrics were
produced with one machine and a couple of workers than with

many hand looms and large numbers of weavers. This gave rise to several grievous incidents in the textile centers of Europe—notably in Lancashire, England, and the areas of Lyon, the Franco-Belgian frontier, and Catalonia. The workers displaced by the machine rioted and burned—or tried to burn—the factories. But they soon came to realize that mechanization reduced the price of the product and left the consumers with money to buy other commodities that formerly had not been within their reach. Producers expanded their enterprises and hired the hands left idle by the introduction of machinery into the textile industry. On the other hand, mechanization in general created in turn a vast industry devoted to the manufacture of machinery that likewise more than absorbed those unable to find work in the factories.

Between 1848 and 1914, unemployment as a mass phenomenon disturbing the whole economy was unknown. Some industries declined, others prospered, and the workers who were discharged from the former found employment in the latter. Besides, as there was at that time complete freedom of migration and of labor throughout the world, those who were not satisfied with the conditions of employment in one country emigrated to wherever wages were higher, and thus a relative prosperity was in the process of being generally diffused.

With the advent of the First World War, conscription and the demands of war production (arms, munitions, clothing, and food—in Germany, for example, eighty per cent of all the production of food and clothing was for the army) resulted in a great scarcity of labor. Taking advantage of this situation, the trade-unions succeeded in forcing wages upward. When the war came to an end, the labor force increased enormously, for the returning soldiers were added to those who had taken their places during the hostilities and had flocked to the factories from the country or from domestic life (women especially), without any corresponding increase in the demand for goods, since every member of the actively employed working population produces for several members of the general population.

But three other factors played a role in this situation. A great part of the labor force created during the war was fitted to work only in war industries, and these had shut down. On the other hand, wages had gone up, while the normalization of production was causing prices to fall, so that these wages now exceeded the value of what the workers were producing. Industrial equipment had been used up, and there was no capital available to replace it, much less to add to it to give work to the unemployed. After all, the war had been immensely destructive. It had impoverished the world, and there was no other recourse but for everyone to restrict his consumption. For the worker this retrenchment had to consist in contenting himself with a lower wage rate, so that the product of his labor could be offered for sale at prices obtainable in an impoverished market.

But this was contrary to the policy of the trade-unions, and the governments found themselves obliged to resort to unemployment benefits to take care of those who had been thrown out of work. As they lacked the money for this, they had to fabricate or create it: the printing presses were set rolling, and there was money for everybody, but devalued money, because prices rose as fast as the supply of money increased. Those workers who were unwilling to accept a direct cut in their wages had them reduced indirectly in the form of monetary devaluation; but, in addition, the unemployed, who could have increased production by accepting lower wages, did not do so and thereby retarded the return to normalcy. Something similar happened after the Second World War. In England, for example, the Labor Government had to devalue the pound sterling, because high wages raised production costs to the point where it became difficult to export.

From what has been said here, it follows that unemployment is not an essential element of what has been improperly called the capitalistic economy. On the contrary: the natural tendency of such an economic system is toward an increase in production and, concomitantly, in jobs. When a new machine produces more goods with less labor, this does not mean that the supernumerary workers are left idle, for they either remain in the same industry tending new machines or transfer to another in greater need of their labor. The characteristic feature of an economy of free enterprise is that it provides work for everybody who wants it and an ever increasing supply of goods and services. But in order for this to occur, it is necessary that there be no interference with production on the part of either pressure groups or the state. If pressure groups exact wages that render production no longer profitable, or if the state imposes on profits taxes that make it impossible for enterprises to maintain or increase their productive equipment, then a brake is put on production, and job opportunities are correspondingly contracted.

Thus, both the theory of so-called "institutional unemployment" and the theory of the "industrial reserve army" of Marx and Engels are quite untenable. According to the first, capitalism always involves periods of general unemployment, and, according to the second theory, unemployment is chronic. Both theories, as we have seen, contradict the facts and the very essence of an economy of free enterprise. There is no unemployment in normal times, much less during a period of prosperity. *There is unemployment when there is a crisis*, i.e., when the action of pressure groups renders production unprofitable by raising costs above market prices. There is also unemployment when the fiscal policies of the government prevent the increase in the accumulation of capital goods from keeping pace with and, if possible, surpassing the increase in the population and thereby raising the general standard of living. Another cause of unemployment is nationalism and its corollary, economic protectionism and migration barriers, which place difficulties in the way of the normal world-wide distribution of goods and services.

Even less tenable is the doctrine given currency a few years before the Second World War by the English economist John Maynard Keynes (later Lord Keynes). Paradoxically, this doctrine attained its greatest popularity precisely at the time when, according to the reports of his intimate friends, Lord Keynes himself was beginning to recognize its falsity, and when he was on the point of making a public declaration to that effect; in any case, he died without having done so. According to this doctrine, unemployment is due to saving and is to be combatted by resorting to every means to force those who have money to spend it—as if bringing money to the market had the magic power of raising up new plants and factories. In reality, the only effect of such a policy is to increase the price of goods and, by the same token, to reduce the general standard of living. Where money is really needed is in *production* for the purchase of more machinery and equipment, the employment of more workers, and the manufacture of more goods for the market with the object of lowering the cost of living. And this is precisely what saving does. He who saves money does not keep it under a mattress, as people did in the mercantilist era, but *invests* it to produce a profit or to yield interest. Either he puts it into real property or into mortgages, and thereby favors the expansion of housing and the employment of construction workers; or he invests it in equities and buys shares of productive enterprises, which are also thus enabled to expand; or he lends it at interest to entrepreneurs, with the same result for the general well-being. Saving and capital accumulation, then, are the great factors making for an increase in production and a consequent abundance of jobs and a lowering of prices. The liquidation of savings, the spending of money in the market in order to acquire consumption goods, has the opposite effect: the stagnation of production, a rise in prices, a diminution in the purchasing power of the general public, a slump, and, consequently, mass unemployment. The Keynesian formula, therefore, leads to results that are exactly contrary to those it is aimed at attaining.

7

International Trade

A quotation from Karl Marx. Caravans and trading posts. The world market. Marts, trades halls and exchanges, fairs and expositions. Commodity exchanges, warrants, and transactions at long distance and involving deferred delivery. Futures. Tribunals of commercial arbitration. Money-changers, bills of exchange, securities, and the stock exchange.

Through its exploitation of the world market, the bourgeoisie has given a cosmopolitan character to production in every country. To the great chagrin of the reactionaries, it has deprived industry of its national character. The old, established national industries have been destroyed or are on the point of being destroyed. They have been supplanted by new industries, whose production poses a vital problem for all civilized nations—industries that no longer process indigenous raw materials, but raw materials bought in the most distant regions and whose products are consumed not only at home, but in every part of the world.

In place of the old wants, satisfied by the products of the country, we find new wants, requiring for their satisfaction the products of the most remote lands and diverse climes. In place of the old national isolation and local self-sufficiency, we have universal trade and the interdependence of nations.

This is how Karl Marx and Friedrich Engels, in their famous *Communist Manifesto* of 1848, describe, in vivid fashion, the economy of their age. But in spite of the fact that Marx did his writing in the library of the British Museum, which at that time was the largest in the world, he was not, it would seem, well versed in history; for even in the most remote eras of antiquity we find the famous *caravans*—already mentioned in the *Thousand and One Nights*—transporting products between the farthest reaches of the Orient and the most distant lands of the Occident then known.

Centuries before Socrates and Plato, Tyrian traders plied their fragile craft as far as the Atlantic coast of the Iberian peninsula. Later, the Greeks and the Phoenicians established *trading posts* along the Mediterranean littoral as far as the mouth of the Rhone, and the Romans, sailing beyond England, penetrated all the way to Ireland.

The Tartars and the Mongols carried on a commercial traffic from the Pacific to the Danube, whence they continued as far as the Baltic and the North Sea. From here the Vikings carried their trade to the coasts of Africa and apparently, as certain competent historians assure us, traversed the icy seas, by way of Bering Strait, to America. Thus, we find in the extreme Orient the most distant products of the Occident, like steel blades from Toledo and the amber of the Baltic; and, on the other hand, the silks, brocades, rugs, jewelry, and perfumes of the Orient found their way as far as England and Sweden.

Even the most cursory perusal of any treatise on commercial geography [1] should suffice to convince one that there has always been a world economy constituting a unified totality. No matter how superficially we survey the daily life of any person, even the least civilized, we shall find that he continually, and without even being aware of it, depends on the products of distant lands. We need hardly mention the machinery produced in the great industrial countries like England, France, Belgium, Germany, and the United States, and dispersed all over the world, or the perfumes of Grasse or the silks of Lyon, which are used by elegant ladies everywhere, or the woolens of Australia, which clothe the middle and the upper classes of every country; nor need we speak of products as local as coffee, tea, and tobacco, which are in universal use, or of the fine woods of the Orient and Central America, which adorn the homes of people in every latitude. In the houses of even the most humble inhabitants of the Orient we shall find cooking utensils and sewing machines manufactured in Europe and the United States, just as we find in the Occident cloves and spices of Oriental provenance and countless knick-knacks from China and Japan.

In a word, the true market is the *world market*. At the center of this market, in the Middle Ages, were the small Italian republics, especially those of Genoa and Venice, and the free cities of the Hanseatic League, as well as their neighbors, the Flemish ports, in particular that of Antwerp. It was here that the characteristic institutions of the world market—the *trades halls* and the *exchanges*—as well as the peculiar forms of mercantile transactions involving operations at a distance and deferred delivery [2] first came into being.

The most primitive form of market is the local *mart* or trading center, which still exists today among almost all the peoples of the world. Later, markets or *fairs* were held regularly, generally every week, in which the indigenous merchandise of the region was offered for sale: cereals, milk products, cattle and meat, certain textiles, household utensils, etc. These were followed later still, not by national, but by international markets, at which traders from all parts of the world would make a stop as they crossed back and forth along the trade routes. These merchants seldom brought with them the goods they had for sale but kept them on deposit in *warehouses*, in ships anchored in the harbor, or on the docks of the so-called *ports of call*. They made their sales by exhibiting samples of their merchandise or simply on the basis of qualitative classifications, which means that what they had to offer consisted of fungible commodities: consumers' goods and raw materials, like fibers and minerals, susceptible of being qualitatively graded and interchangeable within each category. The places where these merchants congregated in Italy and Spain were called, at the end of the Middle Ages and at the beginning of the modern era, *loggias* or *lonjas*. The most ancient of these trades halls are probably those founded by the Catalans in Alexandria and the celebrated *llotja de mar* of

Barcelona of the fourteenth century, still standing in a magnificent Gothic edifice of which a smaller imitation was later made in Valencia. (There is also a French *loge de mer* at Perpignan.) It should not be forgotten that international maritime traffic from the Baltic to Constantinople was regulated for four centuries by the first document having the character of a commercial code, the *Consulado de mar*, apparently drawn up in the thirteenth century at Barcelona, although the first known edition of it dates from 1484.

In the same period, a family of Dutch exchange brokers named Van Burse founded a similar institution in Bruges, whence comes the word "bourse," which passed to Antwerp and into almost all other countries except the Anglo-Saxon. An analogous institution, called the Royal Exchange, was founded in London by Sir Thomas Gresham (whose name has been given to the supposed law—undoubtedly attributable to him, but apparently first formulated by Copernicus—according to which bad money drives good money from the market). In modern times it has once again become the fashion to hold *expositions,* sometimes national, but chiefly international, the most famous of which is the Leipzig trade fair in Germany. At these expositions the articles displayed and traded are not fungible commodities, but almost exclusively manufactured or finished goods, such as, at Leipzig, fine furs, books, machinery, and precision instruments.

The object of the trades halls or *commodity exchanges* is to save space and time. Present in symbolic form, through their owners or the latters' agents, are commodities of the most distant provenance: coffee, tea, sugar, cotton, linen, furs, metals, cereals, etc. The buyers make their purchases from samples or according to graded classifications of quality and receive, not the merchandise itself, but an order for its delivery or simply a negotiable instrument, consisting of an endorsable warehouse receipt, called a *warrant.* Often the merchandise involved in the transaction is never seen, but title to it may be transferred by successive acts of assignment. In this way, transportation over long distances is avoided. Thus, a parcel of cotton coming from the United States and actually arriving at Argentina may have been purchased in

London first by a Portuguese, who then resold it to a Greek, who, in turn, sold it to an Argentinian, the cotton being still in the field all the while.

But time—that great enemy of the entrepreneur—is also saved by means of transactions in *futures,* i.e., present contracts for the purchase or sale of commodities to be delivered at a specified date in the future. This kind of operation makes it possible for the processor of raw materials to be sure that he will have them, at a fixed price, when he needs them and thereby facilitates his calculations in advance of his entering into sales contracts.[3]

Such transactions are usually carried on by means of samples or simply on the basis of qualitative grades (e.g., average Santos coffee, good middling cotton, etc.), in standardized units and at prices that are often little more than approximations based on estimates (e.g., of the alcoholic content of liquids or of the resistance of cotton to twisting, etc.). Both buyer and seller deposit funds as a guarantee of good faith. Since transactions of this kind can give rise to misunderstandings and disputes, the exchanges, and most notably those specializing in particular commodities, have established *international tribunals of commercial arbitration,* to which the contracting parties can submit their case for a decision concerning quality, quantity, and the final terms of settlement. These organs of arbitration, like the one for cotton at Liverpool or New York, for coffee at Le Havre, etc., have justly earned an excellent reputation for their integrity and enjoy a prestige based on universal respect and esteem. Their decisions are recognized by almost all the courts of justice in the world as binding obligations on the contracting parties. The result is that transactions of this kind, apparently the most difficult and perilous, never give rise to insoluble conflicts.

In order to meet the monetary needs of international trade, a *foreign-exchange* market developed. In the early days of international trade, buyers resorted to money-changers to obtain the foreign money demanded by the seller. As the handling of specie proved cumbersome, expensive (because of the costs of transportation and insurance), and dangerous, the *bill of exchange* was

invented. The buyer in Paris who needed pounds sterling paid a
money-changer francs, in exchange for which he received from
the money-changer an order drawn on the latter's London agent
to pay the bearer pounds sterling to the amount shown. If this
bill bore a signature in which the seller had confidence, he accepted it in payment and incurred no risk because it was drawn
to the order of a designated person, who could *endorse* it over
to another person, but it was payable only to the ultimate bearer
whose name appeared last on it.

The person acquiring the bill paid a *premium* for it to the one
who provided him with it, and the amount of this premium remained subject to the law of the market—i.e., of supply and
demand. Those who were in a position to offer such *instruments
of payment* were accustomed to congregate in a certain place,
which was also frequented by those who needed them, and there
competition resulted in the best price for both buyers and sellers.
In Paris these transactions took place as early as the fourteenth
century on the Pont-au-Change. Hence arose the foreign-exchange
or money markets, which later became *stock exchanges* dealing
in all types of securities, because not only was there a need for
instruments of payment, but people also wanted to *invest* money
in *stocks* and *bonds* (loans represented by credit instruments to
which title is transferable, like mortgage debentures) of national
or foreign enterprises or to *place money at interest* by the purchase of government bonds, national or foreign, constituting
claims on the *public debt*. The *prices quoted* for all these different types of securities fluctuated, like those of any commodity,
according to the law of supply and demand, the confidence they
inspired, or the outlook for the future of the companies or governments issuing them. For similar reasons, fluctuations also took
place not only in the premiums charged for instruments of payment in the money market, but also in the rate of foreign exchange itself, and the law of supply and demand always resulted
in the rate of exchange most acceptable to all concerned.

This is what we could characterize as the normal state of
commercial intercourse between nations, and this too is the

mechanism by which it functions. Its enormous advantages are easily conceived. They consist essentially in the fact that every buyer can obtain, almost without leaving his home (because the telephone, the telegraph, and the facilities provided by *exchange brokers* render any personal dislocation unnecessary), anything that he needs, no matter where it comes from. On the other hand, the seller can, also without leaving his home, and even sometimes without seeing his merchandise, have it sent anywhere in the world. The commodity and securities exchanges are mirrors in which are reflected all the vendible goods in the world in their quantity and quality, and where producers find registered the needs and anticipations of people everywhere at any time. This public offer and demand, in free and open competition, automatically eventuates, in the form of market *quotations*, in the prices exactly suited to ensure that the producer will not withdraw from production and that the consumer will not refrain from buying. In a word, thanks to free trade and the efficient service of exchanges and *arbitrage* operations (i.e., conjoined purchases and sales to take advantage of price differentials in differently situated markets), the result is the *best and cheapest world-wide distribution of goods.*

And yet this system has its detractors and has for some time now been in a state of *crisis* because its critics have succeeded in influencing public opinion. Against the world-wide free economy two enemies have arisen: nationalism and socialism; and another enemy disguised as a friend: so-called central planning, or the doctrine of the planned economy. We shall concern ourselves with these three tendencies in the two succeeding chapters.

8

Nationalism and Socialism

Nationalism in antiquity. "Political economy." "National re-
sources." Autarky. The balance of payments and the problem of
"foreign exchange." Dumping, import quotas, and the "black
market." Some verses of Heine. Statistics and the postulate of
abundance. The "unjust distribution of wealth." Expropriation.
The socialist economy. The theory of ground rent and the doc-
trines of Henry George.

Nationalism appears to be a modern phenomenon having
its origin in the nationalities constituted in Europe between the
sixteenth and the nineteenth century concomitantly with the
disappearance of feudalism and of the Romano-Germanic Empire
that came into being with Charlemagne and was totally liquidated
with the unification of Italy. In fact, however, the spirit of
nationalism is very ancient.[1] It has been and still is present as a
factor in both political and economic history. The only thing
that has changed is its form. It was this spirit that animated the
absolutist and totalitarian regime of the Egyptians, that of the
decadent Roman Empire, and the mercantilism of the seventeenth and eighteenth centuries, and, after a brief eclipse that
lasted from the Congress of Vienna to the First World War,
revived in the form of the so-called controlled or planned economy under the combined influence of war and socialism. The
latter system arose as an international movement of the working

class, having as its slogan, "Proletarians of all countries, unite!" but it has since passed to the opposite side and now says, "Proletarians of all countries, don't come to my country and take my job away from me!"

In its economic aspect, nationalism is based on two fallacies: the belief in the existence of national economies and the doctrine that a nation can prosper economically only at the expense of the rest of the world. These convictions were among the first to be combatted by the classical economists, but they were unable to free themselves entirely from the myth of the national economy. Thus, Adam Smith entitled his book *The Wealth of Nations,* and until very recently treatises on economics bore the title "Political Economy," even when they were antinationalistic in content.

Nothing is more illusory than the existence of a national economy and national wealth. Nations do not own any property (the resources at the disposal of governments consist of what they need to perform their functions) and are neither rich nor poor; this is possible only for individuals. In recent years the bureaucratic organs of the League of Nations and latterly of the United Nations have spent vast sums of money on calculating machines, writing materials, books, travel expenses, and salaries for "economists" engaged in computing the wealth and income of nations. All these calculations are utterly fantastic and lead absolutely nowhere, because there is no possible way, no matter how many laws are passed or how powerful a police organization is created, of knowing what each individual who lives in a particular country owns or earns. Each case is unique; the peoples' lack of confidence in their governments is inveterate and founded on bitter experience; and the majority refuse to divulge all that they have hidden in the house or outside the country or to reveal what their true earnings are, even when they are assured that this information is being sought purely for "statistical purposes," because they fear that sooner or later these statistical purposes will turn out to be tax collectors, if not outright expropriators.

After the last war, France—the France of the statisticians—was totally ruined, because the Germans had plundered everything they could lay their hands on. And yet France has revived and is today, in spite of the statistics, a rich country, not because of the American aid provided by the Marshall Plan, much of which was used for bureaucratic expenses and armaments, but simply because the French have made use of their reserves of gold and their foreign assets, which, in spite of the decrees and threats of Marshal Pétain and the Germans, they succeeded in preserving from the general pillage. The country has saved itself by virtue of the refusal of its citizens to allow themselves to be expropriated, by their disobedience of the decrees of stupid or traitorous governments. And the example of France is by no means unique.

No less illusory is the myth of the economic solidarity of the citizens of one country as opposed to the inhabitants of other countries. From what we have already observed of the economic interdependence of all people everywhere, it becomes manifest that it is absurd and impossible for a country to attempt to live in *autarky* exclusively on its own resources. No country, however extensive and diversified it may be, not even Russia or the United States, has at its disposal all the natural resources needed for its production and consumption. All countries have to import, and not on a small scale, food and raw materials as well as manufactured goods, if they are not prepared to content themselves with a miserable subsistence dearly paid for, because there are branches of industry that can produce at low cost only on a large scale or under especially favorable conditions. (As we know from the law of comparative cost and the law of returns, few countries are in a position to produce economically heavy machinery, automobiles, etc.) They need to export in order to pay for their imports.

For this reason, the only really integral economic whole is the international, or rather, the world-wide, market, because, in fact, trade takes place, not between nations, but among men and across national frontiers. This universal economic community can be realized only when every entrepreneur buys and sells in the markets of the whole world. In this way, demand and supply are allowed free play and brought into equilibrium; income and expenses balance each other everywhere quite insensibly, without difficulties or conflicts; and everyone adjusts himself smoothly and imperceptibly to his possibilities. But as soon as national groups, rather than individuals, seek to enter the market, the whole mechanism of commercial intercourse becomes sluggish as well as dangerous, because covetous ambitions, rivalries, and conflicts arise among armed powers.

The slogan, "Buy what the fatherland produces; produce what the fatherland needs," has not been and cannot be of any avail at all, because whoever is in want of a commodity buys it however and wherever he finds it. This, indeed, is the very essence of man's innate faculty of economic judgment and choice. On the other hand, for a country to produce what it needs, natural conditions have to be favorable, and there must be a sufficient demand to make production profitable, for no one will undertake to produce a commodity, no matter how much the country may need it, that economic calculation shows to be unprofitable and incapable of competing on the world market.

But most absurd of all is the obsession that a country can prosper only when it has a favorable *balance of trade*, that is, when it exports more than it imports and receives in income more than it pays out—which is tantamount to saying that a country can prosper only at the expense of other countries. This was, indeed, the favorite argument of the supporters of mercantilism, a policy whose disastrous consequences are very well described in the book by Conrad previously cited. What the exponents of this doctrine fail to realize is that it is impossible to be rich in the midst of poverty, because wealth consists in the possibility of making exchanges. Suppose, for example, that the United States keeps on exporting year after year more than it imports, until it finally accumulates virtually all the money of the other countries, which have been spending all this time in importing more than they have exported and paying the difference in gold. Either the United States will have to use this gold to make further purchases and thereby render its balance of payments "unfavorable," or international commerce will have to be reduced to barter transactions in which the people of the United States will give more than they receive. A country prospers economically when it increases its production of goods that, by their quality and price, are in demand in the world market, and, with the proceeds from such sales, buys in the same market other products which it needs and which are offered for sale by those capable of producing them in abundance at attractive prices.

It is easy to understand that this is possible only when both buyer and seller enjoy full liberty to exercise their initiative, not merely within each country, but across political boundaries. Nations are not economic, but political, communities of men who agree among themselves on the way in which they are to live together. Exercising what the Declaration of Independence calls the right to "the pursuit of happiness," each man in every country undertakes to offer his fellow men all over the world those commodities that suit them by their quality and price, in exchange for which he obtains money; with this he and those who have assisted him in the process of production (for they all receive their share of the remuneration, whether for labor or for capital) buy from other entrepreneurs on the national or international market the commodities they need or want. This freedom of initiative and this desire for constant improvement in well-being is what makes for individual progress and thereby for the progress of national groups, for the latter is nothing but the sum of the advances made by their individual components. When, on the other hand, the activity and initiative of individuals are regulated in view of a supposed *national interest,* stagnation ensues, the rhythm of economic life diminishes, conflicts arise among different groups, force is invoked, and an armed struggle results.

In the period of great economic prosperity that comprised almost the whole of the nineteenth century and the first years of the twentieth, no one concerned himself about the national economy or the balance of payments, a concept first given currency apparently by David Ricardo (previously one spoke only of a commercial balance). Everyone was busy producing goods or services that would find acceptance in the world market; and this multilateral network of productive efforts resulted in a situation in which everything produced was bought and sold, everyone raised his standard of living, and there never was a lack of *foreign exchange*. Indeed, up to 1914, there was not a single case in which anyone in any country wanted to import something and could not do so because he did not have the foreign money needed to pay a reasonable price for it. But one day some German economists, who were more or less in the service of the militarist and imperialist faction, described the existence of what they called the national economy *(Volkswirtschaft)*, began to question whether Germany was receiving a just compensation for the productive efforts of her people, and created a psychological "complex" with regard to international exploitation that led to the war of 1914 and later to that of 1939.

Thereafter, day and night one began to speak of the balance of payments, the statisticians set to work, and we learned that for a long time all countries had been importing more than they exported. This belief led to government intervention in international commerce, import quotas, "dumping" (i.e., subsidized exports), and foreign-exchange controls. The result was that as the intervention was extended and intensified, the deficit in the balance of payments kept on increasing.

Whoever has the patience to peruse the statistics of the various nations will be surprised to find that, all told, more merchandise is imported in the world today than is exported, and that more gold is exported than is imported. Naturally, this is impossible, and the explanation for it is to be found in the fact that these statistics are all incorrect. In the first place, they calculate the value only of those imports and exports that are under control and visible, using the arbitrary prices fixed by the governments for customs purposes. In the second place, these statistics record the movements of foreign exchange (generally today dollars, Swiss francs, or pounds sterling) made through controlled or visible channels; no account is taken of the fact that this movement of goods and money is not the whole of the actual movement, but only a part. This part becomes all the smaller, the greater the extent of government intervention, for the latter creates and feeds the *black market*—that is to say, the true market, since it is the free market. Yet it is on the basis of these statistics that the economic policy of the governments is founded—a mistaken policy that *multiplies* the very evils it is designed to avoid. In fact, actual economic life continues to take its course, but in a form more burdensome to the consumers, who must now pay not only the expenses of the government's intervention, but a premium for the risks incurred on the black market. Thus, the result of the policy of economic nationalism is to make the countries that adopt it, not richer, but poorer, because it inhibits economic activity and raises prices.

Another enemy of the world-wide free market is *socialism*. The labor movement [2] began and developed under the banner of socialism, however many may have been the names—social democracy, syndicalism, collectivism, communism, etc.—given, in the course of the years, to the diverse tendencies that represent but variant expressions of the same fundamental thesis. The word itself seems to have been coined by Robert Owen (1771–1858), an Englishman, to signify that economic activity ought to be inspired exclusively by altruism, and that the economy ought to be social, rather than individualistic. In this connection, one may cite an interesting observation by the Italian economist Pantaleoni, an adherent of the mathematical school, who, in rebutting a criticism that accused him of founding his economic calculations on individual egoism, wrote these words: "You say that we start from the assumption that man is egoistic; but, from the economic point of view, it would make no difference whatsoever if we were to start from the assumption that man is altruistic. Nothing more would be required than a change of sign. For egoistic rivalry will be substituted rivalry in the spirit of sacrifice, and free competition will continue to exist."

The leitmotif of socialism, which runs through all the different variants of proletarian orthodoxy, was expressed in masterly fashion, albeit in terms perhaps not altogether accurate in point of fact, by the German poet Heinrich Heine in the following verses:

> *Ein neues Lied, ein bessres Lied,*
> *Oh Freunde, will ich Euch dichten;*
> *Wir wollen hier auf Erden schon*
> *Das Himmelreich errichten.*
>
> *Wir wollen auf Erden glücklich sein*
> *Und wollen nich mehr darben;*
> *Verschlemmen soll nich der faule Bauch*
> *Was fleissige Händen erwarben.*
>
> *Es giebt auf Erden Brot genug*
> *Für alle Menschenkinder*
> *Und Tulpen und Lilien und Schönheit und*
> *   Lust*
> *Und Zuckererbsen nicht minder.*

Literally translated, these lines may be rendered thus: "I wish to compose a new, a better song for you, my friends. We want to attain to the kingdom of heaven while we are yet here on earth. We want to be happy in this life and not to be in need any more. No lazy wastrel should consume what hard-working hands have acquired. There is enough bread on earth for all mankind, and tulips and lilies and beauty and joy and surgarplums too."

This leitmotif consists, as we see, of two themes: abundance and exploitation. There is, we are told, enough bread and even "sugarplums" on earth for all men, but the "lazy wastrel" is depriving "hard-working hands" of their rightful produce. Nevertheless:

1. The possibilities of acquiring goods, services, and commodities of every kind in a country within a definite period of time—a year, for example—are represented by the total amount of money that its inhabitants have earned in that period. This sum represents the production of the country in the same period of time. The amount spent on things and services, in general, is

the price of these things and services. The annual income of each individual is the numerical expression of his part of the supply of the commodities that are available in that year for the whole population.

Now, according to the annual report of the U.N. for 1953, the most recent date for which we have found comparative statistics, the average annual income per head of the population was $1,800 in the United States, $957 in Switzerland, $705 in Great Britain, $620 in France, $234 in Brazil, and $160 in Japan. In Mexico (according to the book entitled *El desarollo económico de México* compiled by government experts, both Mexican and American, and published by the Fondo de Cultura Económica), the average annual income per head of the population in 1950 was $180 in terms of the money of that year, which was then worth half of what it had been worth in 1930. Recent figures for India are not available, but in 1930 the average annual income per head of the population was less than one-tenth that of Switzerland, which would come to about $70. This would be what each inhabitant of these countries could buy if the national income were divided equally among all, and if it were expended entirely on consumption, without any deduction for taxes or for maintaining the factors of production and increasing them at least in proportion to the increase in the population. In the light of these figures, Heinrich Heine could hardly say today that there is in the world enough for everybody to have not only bread but "sugarplums." Instead, he would agree with the statement of the late Charles Gide, the French economist, that Adam Smith should have entitled his book, not *The Wealth of Nations*, but *The Poverty of Nations*.

2. The United States has the reputation of being the capitalist country par excellence and the one in which the national wealth is most inequitably distributed. Nevertheless, according to the statistics of the Federal Reserve System, 70 per cent of the national income goes to wages and salaries, 20 per cent to professional people, tradesmen, and independent artisans, and only 10 per cent to those receiving interest, dividends, and rents.

Around 1953, the *American Economic Review* published a

study made by the National Bureau of Economic Research which showed that, after taxes, the average annual income of the richest 7 per cent of the population was $3,267 per person and of the remaining 93 per cent of the population $1,124 per person. If the income of the upper 7 per cent were divided equally among the whole population after taxes, each individual of the remaining 93 per cent of the population would receive an additional $150 per year; that is, the average American per capita income would be $1,274 per year instead of $1,124—an increase of somewhat more than 10 per cent.

Professor Lewis [3] comes to the same conclusion in regard to England. If the same coefficient is applied to the rest of the countries mentioned above, the increase in the absolute income of the average Frenchman or Mexican would be even less. With this, they would not only have to live, but they would also have to make provision for industrial investments, and the latter, in a country as little industrialized as Mexico, have amounted in the last few years, according to the book cited above, to around 14 per cent of the national income. In order to maintain these investments, the Mexican, after the division of the total annual output, would be left with an average income less than he actually has at his disposal today, and it is by no means certain that the beneficiaries of such a redistribution in the other countries for which we have cited statistics would not find, in the final analysis, their total income available for consumption likewise diminished.

3. The facts, then, belie the two fundamental theses of the socialist critique of the so-called capitalist economy. The latter, indeed, is no more particularly "capitalist" than any other, for capital, or a stock of producers' goods, on however rudimentary a scale, is and always has been a necessity in every economic system. The domestic silk-spinner and the weaver require distaffs and hand looms; craftsmen and artisans need more or less expensive tools and machines. The same is true of the communist countries. Socialized industries also need fixed and circulating capital; they too have to calculate and adjust their prices, at least of their exports, to those of the world market. It is only

in regard to wages that the communist countries can avoid being made subject to the laws of the market, because wage rates are prescribed by the government, and not exactly in favor of the workers; for, as Joseph E. Davies, the quondam American ambassador to Russia,[4] and Walter Lippman [5] demonstrate, the differences between the wages of the workers and those of the managers are much greater there than in the United States.

In short, the actual economic situation today is characterized, not by abundance, but by scarcity; not by an unjust distribution of wealth, but by inequalities corresponding to differences in productivity.

4. For the alleged *unjust distribution of wealth* socialism, in all its various forms, does not seek corrective measures; this is rather the object of the so-called social reform movements, and more especally of the "planned" or "controlled" economy. Marx formulated the aim of socialism as the *expropriation of the expropriators*. With the so-called *surplus value* that they allegedly withhold for themselves from the total proceeds of the labor of those whom they employ, the capitalists have made themselves owners of the means of production. *They have to be deprived of their ownership of the means of production;* i.e., their mills and factories have to be taken away from them. On whose behalf? On behalf of the people, who will then consist exclusively of workers. How is this to be accomplished? This is the great problem of socialism that Kautsky discusses, without solving it, in his pamphlet entitled *The Day after the Revolution.*[6] In general, two tendencies have manifested themselves. The so-called social democrats advocate that the property of private enterprise pass into the hands of the state as the representative of the people; the followers of Bakunin (the anarchosyndicalists) want it to pass directly into the hands of the workers' councils. The communists envision two distinct stages: a preparatory socialist stage, consisting of the dictatorship of the proletariat, with production centralized by the state, and true communism, in which the state will "wither away," leaving only the workers' councils.

What is not seen clearly and has not been explained by anybody is what difference all this would make in comparison with the system of free enterprise or what advantage the workers would derive from such a change. Production would continue to be capitalistic and subject to the laws of the market, which, in an economy operated by the state, would condition the prices of imported and exported products, and consequently of all the rest. In a syndicalist economy the free play of competition would be even more complete. From the prices imposed by the market would have to be deducted costs of production, financial charges, and reinvestments for the maintenance and expansion of the capital structure. The direction of commerce and technology would require a differential compensation such as is, in fact, demanded and received in Russia. The remainder would be left for the workers, as at present, but with these two differences in their disfavor. In the first place, those responsible for the conduct of business, not being entrepreneurs, would neither reap profits nor suffer losses; they would be assured their own salaries, and the remainder would be left for the ordinary workers. This is precisely the opposite of what happens under present conditions, in which the fixed remuneration is that of the worker, and the boss keeps the remainder, if there is any. In the second place, under a socialist system, freedom of labor would disappear. In the absence of a labor market, wages would be fixed by the ukase of the monopolistic employer. The right of workingmen to form unions and to go on strike would be suppressed, and the worker would become a slave. This is what is happening in Russia today, where the worker cannot choose even his place of employment, and every effort on his part to improve his condition is punished as high treason.

A very peculiar variety of socialism is *agrarian socialism,* known also as Georgism and as the agrarian reform movement.[7] It bases itself on the theory of *ground rent,* already in germinal form in the works of Adam Smith, Anderson, and Malthus, and developed by David Ricardo. According to this doctrine, when fertile land is abundant, it does not produce any profit, and the prices of the products are measured by the costs of production. But when the population increases, land of the first quality is no longer sufficient to produce the food needed, and recourse has to be taken to land of increasingly inferior quality. The prices of the products then rise by an amount equivalent to the cost of cultivating the poorer land. Those who retain possession of the better land profit from this situation by obtaining prices greater than their costs of production and gain a profit that includes, over and above the normal revenue, a premium, called *ground rent*, in consideration of the superior quality of their own land.

Shortly after the death of Ricardo, an American, Henry George, made full use of this doctrine and developed it in his famous book, *Progress and Poverty*, which has been translated into many languages. He contended that the poverty of the masses is due, not to the exploitation of the industrial worker, but to the monopoly of ground rent enjoyed by the landlords. He therefore proposed, by means of a *single tax*, to confiscate this rent. No country has actually made this attempt, although progressive taxation and differences in tax rates based on ownership of real property have been founded on this theory.

The attempts at agrarian reform made in almost all the countries of Europe after the First World War were directed chiefly against the owners of large landed estates and consisted in the expropriation of the landlords, with or without compensation, and the division of the land so as to increase small holdings. Nevertheless, Henry George had and still has many adherents, and, up to the last world war, there were in several countries agrarian reform movements. Very important among them was that headed by Adolf Damaschke, who was the candidate opposing Hindenberg for the presidency of the German Republic. Damaschke, whose book has been cited above, extended the theory of Henry George to urban property and succeeded in having a *surplus-value tax* imposed on owners of cultivated land that was sold at a high price for the expansion of urban centers. This tax was later adopted by several countries. In recent years Dr. Carlos P. Carranza has defended and developed this theory in a very interesting way.[8]

The doctrine of ground rent is based on two errors, one factual and the other theoretical. The first is the scarcity of land of first-rate quality. This scarcity has become especially noticeable in Europe as a result of overpopulation and the restrictions imposed on immigration in the comparatively less intensively cultivated countries. In reality, there are still in the world vast areas of land of first-rate quality that have not yet been cultivated, as the famous explorer Earl Parker Hanson shows in his very interesting book, *New Worlds Emerging;* [9] and, as a French economist has recently observed, it is absurd that these lands are still not under cultivation, and that large sums of money are being spent on freight costs to supply the overpopulated countries, when it would be better for everybody if the excess population of these countries could migrate to the idle lands, cultivate them, and live off their produce. In the second place, as Ludwig von Mises has pointed out,[10] land is nothing but a factor of production like machinery or tools. One may not speak simply of land in general, but of land of different quality and productivity, just as one must take account of machines or tools of different quality, and the owner of a superior machine or tool also can be said to derive a differential "rent" from it in comparison with the returns yielded by inferior equipment. This is why they command different prices in the market, and it cannot be said that the owner of land of good quality whose rent has already been capitalized in the higher price paid for it derives an unearned increment from its exploitation.

9

The Controlled Economy

The origin of the modern planned economy. The "weaknesses"
of the system of free enterprise and their supposed remedies. The
"lack of mobility of resources." The "unjust distribution of
wealth." Redistribution and confiscation. Government control
of prices and wages. Foreign-exchange controls and restrictions
on international trade. Planning in the backward countries. Plan-
ning and communism.

During the First World War the governments of the bel-
ligerent countries as well as of some neutral countries demanded
of their parliaments the power to interfere in economic affairs.
They justified these demands on such grounds as military secrecy,
the priorities required by the war effort, and, in the neutral
countries, the necessity of parrying the blows that the violence
of the conflict was directing against normal economic life in
the form of scarcity and high prices. After the war, came the
return to normalcy, with all its attendant problems, and the
supervening crises.

The waters, it seemed, would not return to their accustomed,
peaceful courses, and in Germany the word *Planwirtschaft* made
its appearance. Oblivious of the origin of the disorder, people
said that the modern economy is too complicated to be allowed
to go its way all by itself; it was necessary for "experts" to draw
up plans and for the governments to put them into effect. There

was no dearth of experts nor of governments desirous of extending the sphere of their authority nor of bureaucrats ready to take advantage of opportunities for easy and well-paid jobs in the new offices that governmental intervention in economic affairs required. There followed a veritable flood of books on the *controlled economy* or *economic planning*. Franklin D. Roosevelt embarked on the New Deal in the United States, with results absolutely spectacular and deceptive.[1] Lord Keynes published his *General Theory of Employment, Interest and Money*,[2] the schools of economics produced at top speed generations of pedantic "economists" who saw the way to paradise in the unending expansion of the civil service, and the world was overwhelmed by an epidemic of government "controls" that recalled the dreadful outbreak of influenza that also followed the First World War.

The "planners" want, so they say, to save the system of free enterprise; yet in fact they are themselves, as Friedrich von Hayek has demonstrated in his famous book, *The Road to Serfdom*,[3] the—albeit in many cases unwitting—harbingers of communism. Their aim, as stated by W. A. Lewis,[4] is to remedy the "weaknesses" of the system of free enterprise, which allegedly consist in the lack of mobility of resources, the unjust distribution of wealth, and the absence of equilibrium in international trade. The remedies proposed for these "weaknesses" are, briefly, taxes and subsidies, government intervention to fix wages and prices, foreign-exchange controls, and restrictions on international trade.

It is proposed that the alleged lack of mobility of resources be corrected by the imposition of taxes on *idle money* that does not find its way into the market and by means of subsidies for *essential industries*. The first is the remedy of Keynesianism, and the second is the policy of *expansionism*. Measures that succeed in stimulating people to buy have the effect of pushing up commodity prices and inducing a rise in the cost of living, because if more money finds its way into the market without any concomitant increase in the supply of goods available, the latter rise in price. On the other hand, the money that is offered for these goods in the market does not go into investments: it is not used to build houses or to increase industrial installations, both of which are prerequisites of an increase in the standard of living. What is needed to bring about an improvement in people's well-being is to bring, not more money into the market, but more goods that can be bought with the same amount of money or even with less, if that is possible.

Hence, it is considered necessary to complement this policy by stimulating production. No account is taken of the fact that the best way of accomplishing this end is to provide an incentive for money to enter production rather than to enter the market for consumers' goods. Instead, what is done is exactly the contrary. And then, for lack of private resources, public funds must be allocated to production; that is, instead of channeling into productive enterprises the money of those who have saved it, what is used for this purpose is public funds, which, in the last analysis, have to be taken away from the consumers. The latter, as a result of this combination of policies, lose both ways: through the increase in prices and through the taxes designed to pay for the subsidies. And when the taxes imposed on the consumers do not produce enough revenue, the governments resort to inflation and a policy of currency expansion, thereby imposing an additional burden on the consumer, because it makes his money worth less.

Thus, the money that was supposed to be withdrawn from saving and investment in order to enter the market for consumers' goods finally finds its way into investment anyway through taxes and inflation, but it does not do so by way of the normal channels. Instead, the government is given discretionary power to dispose of private property as it sees fit and, in effect, to direct production in accordance with plans inspired by utopian economic ideas or, what is worse and no less frequent, by concern for the interests of pressure groups. What is produced is no longer what the consumer demands, but what the government wants; and the consumer finds himself deprived of his right to choose, that is, of his liberty, guaranteed by the constitution, but in fact taken away by the government and replaced by a state of tutelage.

Let us next turn our attention to the so-called *unjust distribution of wealth*. Efforts to correct this supposed unjust distribution are made sometimes by way of taxation and sometimes by way of government interference in the determination of wage rates and prices.

State intervention by way of taxation is of either a corrective or a confiscatory character. In regard to the first, Professor Lewis says that in England twenty per cent of the national income goes to two per cent of the population, that this is excessive, and that half of the income of this minority should be taken away by taxation. He fails to take into account three facts:

1. These so-called privileged people are also the ones who already pay the greater part of the taxes without needing to be especially singled out for this purpose.

2. Most of what they earn they do not consume, because the capacity for consumption is limited, however prodigal and extravagant may be its scale (though in that case, according to Keynes, it performs a useful service for society, because it brings money to the market). Their earnings go chiefly into investments: the construction of houses and the production of goods and services beneficial to the community and tending to raise and improve the general standard of living.

3. The *redistribution* of this surplus would not result in any appreciable gain for those in the lower income brackets (scarcely ten per cent, in fact), and, on the other hand, the money so distributed would find its way into the market for consumers' goods and raise their prices, while being withdrawn from investments. The effect of such a policy must be to make commodities even scarcer and prices even higher than they already are.

Nevertheless, Lewis and those of his persuasion, not content with such measures, go on to propose the outright *confiscation of capital*. They want to take capital out of private hands by means of confiscatory legislation and turn it over to the government. And what would the government do with the money? It can do only one of two things: either spend it in an unproductive way (e.g., by expanding the bureaucracy and the police force or embarking on a questionable program of public works), in which case production is curbed while the population continues to increase and the general standard of living falls; or else employ the money in production directly or through so-called semipublic or "autonomous" agencies, which, for all practical purposes, is socialism—the very thing that the protagonists of a controlled economy profess to wish to avoid with their measures to correct the "weaknesses of a free economy."

Along these same lines, and "to mitigate the sufferings of the poor," the advocates of a controlled economy propose to redistribute wealth through the control of prices and wages— but not of all prices and wages, for that would be socialism, which, they say, they wish to avoid. They want to fix the prices of *essential articles of consumption* that might otherwise sometimes be out of reach of the poor. But this project, so well-intentioned in theory, proves impossible in practice. No producer will be willing to continue in an unprofitable line of production, for it must be remembered that commodities are expensive, not because of the whim of the producer—free competition takes care of that—but because of their costs of production. If the government fixes prices below costs, the producer either will cease production entirely or will have to be subsidized. And as the subsidies are paid by the government out of the public treasury, the result is that what the consumer saves in price he pays in taxes. On the other hand, the very cheapness of a product leads to its more prodigal consumption, and it soon becomes necessary to resort to a policy of *rationing*. But this too fails to solve the problem. When there is rationing, everyone makes sure to take the full amount of his allotted quota even if he does not need it, for in that case he can resell it in the black market or use it for less urgent needs, such as feeding cattle the bread rationed for human consumption. At the end of the last war, when the policy of bread-rationing was abandoned in France, the government was surprised to find that in a free market the French consumed less bread than when it was rationed.

It is less feasible to fix wage rates. Even Lewis recognizes, for example, that a general increase in wages is futile, because it inevitably gives rise to a corresponding, and sometimes greater, increase in prices. Nevertheless, he insists that wage rates be raised in those cases in which they are too low. But when this happens, it is precisely because market prices do not allow of higher wages, since the commodities in question are in abundant supply. If, in such circumstances, wage rates are raised, production becomes unprofitable, the industry in question disappears, the market is deprived of its product, and the workers engaged in its production, finding themselves unemployed, enter the competition for jobs in other industries, whose wage rates they thereby depress.

General monetary controls will not concern us here. But there is a special type of monetary control—*foreign-exchange control* —that, for all practical purposes, is nothing but a particular method of controlling international trade.

The control of international trade is characteristic of tendencies toward both nationalism and socialism. It began almost simultaneously in the Soviet Union and in nationalist Germany. There is nothing extraordinary in this, since nationalism inevitably leads to socialism, and socialism to nationalism. Practically every socialist regime has to be nationalist, and vice versa: in either case what is involved is simply a form of *totalitarianism*. It is not possible to put a nationalist economic policy into effect without taking over control of production and distribution, and this is what socialism is essentially. On the other hand, it is impossible to take over control of production and distribution without inevitably putting into effect a policy of economic nationalism. In both cases there is but one producer and distributor, viz., the state. Sometimes, as in the Germany of Hitler and the Italy of Mussolini, the appearance of an economy of free enterprise is kept up, but in fact it is not that at all, because the producer and the distributor have no other alternative than to obey the regulations established by the state. As a German industrialist said during the Hitler era, "The difference between Russia and Germany consists in the fact that in Russia

the producer is a bureaucrat who neither reaps profits nor
suffers losses, whereas in Germany he is a bureaucrat who only
suffers losses."

The advocates of a controlled economy become indignant
when they are accused of being nationalists and socialists and
consider themselves the saviors of free enterprise in a period of
crisis. They recognize, as does Professor Lewis, the superiority
of international exchange on the world market under a regime
of free, private enterprise, but they nevertheless champion a
policy of government intervention because they have not been
able to liberate themselves from the myth of the *Volkswirtschaft*.
The international free economy is the best, says Professor Lewis,
but it "needs to be strengthened" by means of government intervention in order to maintain an *equilibrium in the balance of
payments*. And what can the state do to maintain this equilibrium?

It is not possible, says Professor Lewis, to attain equilibrium
by restricting imports.

National income cannot be increased by avoiding imports, since this
will result only in diverting resources to the production of articles
of domestic consumption, thereby withdrawing them from the most
profitable export markets. Nor can domestic employment be increased
by reducing imports because this would reduce exports to the same
extent.

His solution is, like that of all the advocates of planning, neither
to restrict nor expand international commerce as a whole, but to
divert it by facilitating or impeding certain imports and exports
in order to bring about corrective adjustments dictated by
political or ideological considerations. The method chosen for
accomplishing this end is foreign-exchange control. There are
many varieties of foreign-exchange control, but it consists essentially in the state's collecting the price of exports and paying for
imports, on behalf of the interested parties, in sound money
(gold or dollars), but paying the exporter and recovering from
the importer an arbitrarily determined amount in the national
currency.

In sum, imports are paid for with the proceeds from exports, and the former extend only as far as the latter permit, exactly as in a free economy. The only difference is that in this case neither the importer nor the exporter is a free agent in carrying on his business, nor does either one of them receive or pay the world market price, but an arbitrarily set price. The distribution thereby effected is unjust and discriminatory, besides being burdened with the expenses of government intervention. Hence, this system of intervention does not succeed in achieving either a more equitable distribution of wealth or a greater mobility of goods and labor or even an increase in international trade. On the contrary, such state intervention is unnecessary, costly, arbitrarily discriminatory, and extremely detrimental to individual liberty.

From this brief exposition of the principles underlying the controlled economy two conclusions clearly emerge: (1) They in no way succeed in avoiding the "weaknesses of a free economy." (2) They produce, instead, new evils, viz., scarcity, high prices, and the suppression of individual liberty. Nevertheless, as a last line of defense, it is proposed that they be applied to the so-called *backward countries.*

Thus, Earl Parker Hanson, the great explorer,[5] believes in the economy of free enterprise, but recommends, nevertheless, a planned economy for the backward countries in order to accelerate their progress without waiting for them to undergo the normal development that individual initiative would bring about.

Interesting in this respect is the opinion of Lewis, himself an advocate of economic planning, as expressed in his little book on the subject, so often cited here, in which there is an appendix especially devoted to a consideration of this question. He says there:

. . . . planning requires a strong, competent, and incorrupt government. . . . .

Now a strong, competent, and incorrupt administration is just what no backward country possesses, and, in the absence of such an administration, it is often much better that governments should be laissez faire than that they pretend to plan. . . . .

But the difficulty which faces these governments is that they cannot expand their own services unless they can raise money to pay for them, and they cannot raise all the money they need because their peoples are too poor. . . . .

If governments of backward countries try to finance their investments by creating money, they will cause an inflation. . . . .

Foreign capital cannot be avoided, even if the government decides to build and operate all the plants itself. The machinery must come from abroad; . . . . backward countries are too poor to be able to provide much capital simply by cutting down luxuries. If they are to industrialize themselves substantially, they have either to cut severely the consumption of necessaries, or else to borrow abroad. A ruthless dictatorship can cut consumption to the desired extent, but a democracy will always have to rely largely on foreign capital. . . . .

And he concludes as follows:

It can thus be seen that planning in backward countries imposes much bigger tasks on governments than does planning in advanced countries. . . . . For, if the people are, on their side, nationalistic, conscious of their backwardness, and anxious to progress, they willingly bear great hardships and tolerate many mistakes. . . . . Popular enthusiasm is both the lubricating oil of planning, and the petrol of economic development. . . . . We can understand the claims of Russia in the 1930's or of Jugoslavia today to have awakened this dynamic enthusiasm. . . . .[6]

But what does it all lead to in the end? Is not Hayek right when he says, in his *The Road to Serfdom*, that the controlled economy drifts inevitably toward communism?

The policy of economic planning, then, is absolutely untenable theoretically; but, besides, in spite of the great prestige that it still enjoys, especially in the economically less important countries (while those in which it was first introduced, like Germany, England, France, and the United States, are abandoning it), its material collapse is only a matter of time. As Professor von Mises appropriately puts it, the countries that are committed to a program of economic planning are giving their peoples the illusion of prosperity at the price of liquidating their reserves. When these are exhausted, a great catastrophe is inevitable unless the people open their eyes before they fall over the precipice.[7]

10

What Economics Is Not About

Production, distribution, and consumption. Equilibrium. Homo economicus. Types of "business associations." Social justice.

We have seen briefly how the economy is constituted by the exercise of man's innate faculty of choice, how it functions when it is allowed to operate freely, how it reacts when it is hampered, and how it can be understood, not by resorting either to arbitrary dogmatism or to merely routine factual description, but by means of critical reflection directed toward the discovery not only of apparent regularities in the phenomena under observation but also of the conditions determining their occurrence. Let us now glance briefly and in very summary fashion at what economics is *not* about.

Let us take any of the best-known treatises of economics: the *Principles* of Charles Gide,[1] a highly esteemed work of which thousands and thousands of copies have been printed in France and many other countries; the *Grundriss der politischen Oekonomie* of Philippovich,[2] a fundamental textbook in the education of so many German and foreign economists; the well-known treatises of Benham,[3] Lutz,[4] Cannan;[5] and even that of the English mathematical economist Marshall[6] or the little manual by his disciple, Chapman;[7] etc., etc. All of them, to a greater or lesser extent, treat production, distribution, and consumption as separate things that have almost nothing to do with one another. Yet the economy cannot be understood in this fashion; for production, distribution, and consumption are not three independent activities nor even three separable phases of a process that can be examined by themselves or by means of a provisional abstraction made for purposes of study or instruction.

The economic process is an integral and continuous whole in which production, distribution, and consumption are essentially concurrent and coincident, so that it is not even intellectually possible to focus attention on any one of these phases to the exclusion of the others. Especially since credit has become generally available, he who produces anything is, in the very process, already distributing what is produced among the human factors of production, and the latter are consuming their respective shares, and so on successively. Production, distribution, and consumption are phases of the same cycle, which repeats itself, but never in identical form. Thus, the economic process is a succession of acts of production, distribution, and consumption, not in the form of successive or concentric circles, but in the form of a spiral. The economic process is living and dynamic: it never repeats itself exactly; it always moves on to a new position.

Hence, the attachment of so many economists for the *evenly rotating economy* is utopian rather than scientific. This was also the ideal of the classical economists and continues to be that of many economists who consider themselves liberals, to say nothing of those who profess themselves adherents of the different varieties of "welfare" or "labor" economics. This longing for a condition of static and beatific tranquillity is essentially reactionary. It is in conflict with the very essence of economic life and, indeed, of human life in general. It seeks, in the words of Heine's poem, to turn the world into a paradise, but turns it instead, to use Abraham Lincoln's apt expression, into a hell by choking off initiative and putting creativity into a straitjacket. The hallmark of all attempts to achieve economic stability is always rationing and coercion; it is essentially static and quantitative, whereas man's faculty of choice, as exercised in regard to economic goods, is essentially dynamic and qualitative.

The essential principle of the economic process is not equilibrium, but disequilibrium. Equilibrium would bring about economic stagnation and death; disequilibrium is the motive force that keeps the economy alive and progressive. Economic life is not a condition of peace and security; it involves daring and adventure. There is no such thing as exact economic calculation, as some mathematical economists have maintained, because the economic data that are at our disposal always refer to the past, and we do not know what tomorrow will bring. Every economic activity is a bill presented to the future, and there is always a question whether or not it will be paid. One could say of economic life what Goethe says at the end of the second part of *Faust:*

> *Alles Vergängliche*
> *Ist nur ein Gleichnis;*
> *Das Unzulängliche,*
> *Hier wird's Ereignis;*
> *Das Unbeschreibliche,*
> *Hier ist es getan* [8]

That is to say:

> All we see before us passing
> Sign and symbol is alone;
> Here, what thought could never reach to
> Is by semblances made known;
> What man's words may never utter
> Done in act—in symbol shown.[9]

Economics is not about anything that could be expressed in mathematical terms; its domain is rather that of imagination and invention, of adventure into the unknown, of a hazardous enterprise that is not for the cowardly.

Hence, it is no less necessary to banish from economics the classical myth of the *homo economicus*. Man is, to be sure, an egoistic being; such is his earthly lot, for no other mode of existence is possible to him; he is actuated by the instinct of self-preservation. But egoism is not the same as avarice; it is, rather, the desire for well-being. And well-being is not always expressible in terms of material goods.

The exercise of man's faculty of choice, which is the pivot on which the whole of economic life turns, is not confined to the kind of goods that are bought and sold in the market. Sometimes the objects of man's preference have no exchange-value at all. A worker prefers, at certain times, leisure, from which he derives no material benefit, to well-paid labor. An engineer who could earn a great deal of money by productive employment for the market prefers to live in a secluded hovel, in the utmost poverty, in order to solve some baffling scientific problem; this makes him happier, just as the laborer mentioned above was made happier by leisure than by paid employment. Or a nabob leaves his fortune to his family or gives it to the poor in order to go and preach the Gospel. We know of a notary who was earning large sums of money in the practice of his profession and abandoned it to become a monk, and of the owner of a great newspaper who left it to become a priest. And there are also cases in which the opposite occurs, and we find old clerics and philosophers turned into captains of industry.

Now these cases that we have cited are not instances of altruism in opposition to the egoism of the entrepreneur. They too are cases of egoism, for everyone who seeks his own happiness is egoistic. Some find it in money, others in science, and still others in simple renunciation. All exercise their faculty of choice.

Hence, in the market, if we may be permitted to use the expression, there is competition not only among vendible goods, but also among things that are, as we commonly say, "beyond price." There is no such being as an "economic man" or a "noneconomic man"; there are only men who exercise the faculty of choice, sometimes preferring vendible goods, sometimes goods without any exchange-value.

The latter are a more important factor in economic life than is generally believed. They are some of the many unknown facts about the future that make economic calculation such a hazardous adventure. The retirement of an entrepreneur of genial disposition can bring fortune or misfortune to many other entrepreneurs, just as the indifference of a truth-seeker to monetary considerations can, at a given moment, make both him and others wealthy.

There are many other things which one finds in treatises on economics, but which likewise have nothing to do with the subject. In many of them we find pages and pages devoted to corporations, trusts, cartels, mergers, and other forms of business associations, combinations, and "communities of interest." These matters have nothing whatever to do with economics; they are strictly legal questions connected with the technical problems of organizing business. Neither is economics concerned with the problem of *costs,* which is so much in vogue at the moment. So-called "costs" economics is nothing but a branch of industrial calculation, and one of lesser importance than is commonly believed, because it is only of auxiliary value to the entrepreneur; his economic calculation, however many data the study of costs provides him with, always has to contend with an unknown factor that will, in any case, render it essentially inexact and hazardous: tomorrow, time, the *future.*

But if there is anything that, above all else, has nothing to do with economics, it is the question of the "just distribution" of wealth, or what is called today, in a phrase that is as seductive as it is empty, "social justice." To speak of social justice or of the just or unjust distribution of resources is like speaking of surrealist astronomy or of musical chemistry, because justice and the conduct of economic affairs are entirely distinct matters, neither related nor opposed, but simply indifferent to each other. The goal of economic activity is a continual increase in the production of commodities, and the only just distribution of resources is that which best serves to attain this end. All that "just" means, at bottom, is "fit," "suitable," "appropriate." The aim of justice, properly so called, is, as the Romans used to say, *to give each his due (ius suum cuique tribuendi),* and in order for each to be given what is his, it is necessary that *it already* belong to him; to "give," in this sense, means to *protect the right of possession*. Each man gets "what belongs to him" in the course of voluntary exchanges that constitute the economic process, and, by virtue of the operation of the market, each receives for his contribution precisely the amount that will impel him to increase the supply of the most urgently demanded commodities. Thus, each one ends by getting his due only when he finally obtains it at the completion of a cycle in the economic process, and precisely by virtue of this process and nothing more. Only when each man thereby gets what belongs to him, and someone wants to take it away from him, does a question of justice arise, and not before.

"But," it will be said, "even though this economic process of constantly increasing the supply of goods and services may, on the whole and in the long run, be able to resolve the problem of providing for the needs of everybody, yet in subjecting men to its own requirements, it could become, at certain times, a veritable Procrustean bed for some of them by imposing on them conditions harder than they could bear. Ought society to remain indifferent to such conditions and console the victims by telling them that later on they or their descendants will be rolling in wealth?" Evidently not, but this is not an economic problem; it is a moral problem—a problem of human solidarity. But why seek to solve it only by political means—by passing laws and establishing governmental institutions? We are here in the realm of public opinion, of education, and, above all, of the example set by the elite. These are the forces that can solve the grave problems of relief and security, by leaving to the interested parties, in free association, the responsibility of managing as they think best the resources they decide to pool in voluntary, co-operative institutions designed with these ends in view. There is no more reason for the state to intervene in such matters than in the economic sphere. When it does so, under the pretext that no confidence is to be placed in individual initiative, it simply deprives men of their constitutional rights and liberties without giving them anything but an illusory security and substitutes government omnipotence for the democratic system.

Notes

NOTES TO CHAPTER 1

1. Heinrich Cunow, *Allgemeine Wirtschaftsgeschichte; eine übersicht über die Wirtschaftsentwicklung von der primitiven Sammelwirtschaft bis zum Hochkapitalismus* (Berlin: J. H. W. Dietz Nachfolger, 1926–1931).
2. We follow here Joseph Conrad, *Historia de la economía* (Spanish translation from the German published by Librerías de Victoriano Suárez, Madrid, and Agustín Bosch, Barcelona).
3. *See* Thomas S. Ashton, *The Industrial Revolution* (London: A. & C. Black, Ltd., 1937).
4. Karl Fuchs, *Volkswirtschaftslehre* (Berlin: W. de Gruyter & Co., 1925).
5. See chap. 3.
6. New Haven: Yale University Press, 1949.
7. Chicago: Chicago University Press, 1944.
8. New York and London: Harper & Brothers, 1946; Irvington-on-Hudson, New York: Foundation for Economic Education, 1952.
9. See chap. 9.

NOTE TO CHAPTER 2

1. *Op. cit.*, p. 195.

NOTES TO CHAPTER 4

1. Gen. 3:17, 19.
2. Joseph E. Davies, *Mission to Moscow* (New York: Simon and Schuster, 1941).

NOTES TO CHAPTER 6

1. Spanish Penal Code of 1870, Article 555. For recent reforms of a similar nature in Mexico, see Article 253 of the Penal Code of the Federal District and Territories. Similar provisions may be found in the French Penal Code, Article 419.
2. *Vieja y nueva economía política* (Buenos Aires, 1954).
3. William Arthur Lewis, *The Principles of Economic Planning* (London: George Allen & Unwin, Ltd., 1949).

NOTES TO CHAPTER 7

1. *See*, for example, Marion Isabel Newbigin, *Commercial Geography* (New York: Henry Holt and Company, 1924).
2. Wilhelm Lexis, *Allgemeine Volkswirtschaftslehre* (Berlin: B. G. Teubner, 1910).

3. *See* A. Gabarró García, *El sistema de futuros* (Barcelona, 1934) and Charles Rist, *Précis des mécanismes économiques élémentaires* (Paris: Librairie du Recueil Sirey, 1945).

NOTES TO CHAPTER 8

1. Riedmatten, *L'Économie dirigée, expériences depuis les pharaons jusqu'à nos jours* (Versailles: Édition l'Observateur, 1948).
2. For a rapid survey of the doctrines and the history of the labor movement, *see* Heinrich Herkner, *Die Arbeiterfrage. Eine Einführung* (Berlin: W. de Gruyter and Co., 1921); Ramsay MacDonald, *Socialism: Critical and Constructive* (London: Cassell and Co., Ltd., 1921); and, for what concerns the international movement, my own *El socialismo y la guerra* (Barcelona: Estudio, 1915).
3. *Op. cit.*
4. *Op. cit.*
5. *The Good Society* (Boston: Little, Brown and Co., 1937).
6. Karl Kautsky, *Das Weitertreiben der Revolution* (Berlin: Arbeitsgemeinschaft für staatsbürgerliche und wirtschaftsliche Bildung, 1920).
7. Adolf Wilhelm Ferdinand Damaschke, *Die Bodenreform* (Jena: G. Fischer, 1913).
8. *Op. cit.*
9. New York: Duell, Sloan and Pearce, 1949.
10. *Human Action: A Treatise on Economics* (New Haven: Yale University Press, 1949), pp. 631 ff.

NOTES TO CHAPTER 9

1. *See* Isabel Leighton, ed., *The Aspirin Age, 1919–1941* (New York: Simon and Schuster, 1949) and John Thomas Flynn, *The Roosevelt Myth* (New York: Devin-Adair Co., 1948).
2. New York: Harcourt, Brace and Co., 1936.
3. Friedrich August von Hayek, *The Road to Serfdom* (Chicago: University of Chicago Press, 1944).
4. *Op. cit.*
5. *Op. cit.*
6. *Op. cit.*, pp. 121 *et seq.*
7. Cf. *Human Action*, p. 847.*

* [In both the original Spanish-language edition and the French translation the equivalent of the passage in the text is enclosed in quotation marks and attributed, without page reference, to Ludwig von Mises' *Human Action*, as if it were a verbatim translation from that book. Although the sentiments expressed in the passage are certainly in accord with the views expounded in *Human Action*, especially on the page cited above, nothing quite corresponding to these sentences can be found in it.—TRANSLATOR.]

NOTES TO CHAPTER 10

1. *Cours d'économie politique* (Paris: L. Larose & L. Terrin, 1918–1920), 2 vols.
2. Tübingen: J. C. B. Mohr, 1893–1907, 3 vols.
3. Frederic C. Benham, *Economics* (New York: Pitman Publishing Co., 1941).
4. Harley Leist Lutz and Benjamin F. Stanton, *An Introduction to Economics* (Chicago; New York: Row, Peterson and Co., 1923).
5. Edwin Cannan, *Elementary Political Economy* (London, 1881) and *A Review of Economic Theory* (London: P. S. King and Son, Ltd., 1929).
6. Alfred Marshall, *Principles of Economics* (London: Macmillan, 1922).
7. Sir Sidney John Chapman, *Elementary Economics* (London: Longmans, Green and Co., Ltd., 1926). Also see his somewhat lengthier *Political Economy* (London: Williams and Norgate, 1912).
8. Part II, Act V *(Himmel)*.
9. *The Second Part of Goethe's "Faust,"* trans. by John Anster (London: George Routledge and Sons, 1886), p. 287.

Index

Prepared by Vernelia A. Crawford

Note: This index includes the titles of chapters, each listed under the appropriate subject classification. With the exception of these specific page references, which are inclusive, the numbers in each instance refer to the *first* page of a discussion. A page number followed by a figure in parentheses indicates the number of a footnote reference.

Recent FEE Publications

Leonard E. Read 256 pages	*Anything That's Peaceful* 2nd printing, Sept. 1993
FEE Classic 206 pages	*Taxation and Confiscation* October 1993
FEE Classic 174 pages	*Bankers and Regulators* November 1993
Lawrence W. Reed 86 pages	*A Lesson From the Past:* *The Silver Panic of 1893* December 1993
Faustino Ballvé 109 pages	*Essentials of Economics* 2nd English ed., Jan. 1994
Edmund A. Opitz 272 pages	*Religion: Foundation of a* *Free Society* February 1994
FEE Classic 164 pages	*American Unionism:* *Fallacies and Follies* March 1994
Mark Spangler, ed. 302 pages	*Clichés of Politics* March 1994
Tibor R. Machan 130 pages	*The Virtue of Liberty* April 1994
Burton Folsom, Jr., ed. 176 pages	*The Spirit of Freedom:* *Essays in American History* May 1994

For a free copy of FEE's latest catalogue of more than 400 titles, contact:

The Foundation for Economic Education
30 South Broadway
Irvington-on-Hudson, New York 10533
telephone (914) 591-7230
fax: (914) 591-8910

About the Publisher

The Foundation for Economic Education, Inc., was established in 1946 by Leonard E. Read to study and advance the moral and intellectual rationale for a free society.

The Foundation publishes *The Freeman*, an award-winning monthly journal of ideas in the fields of economics, history, and moral philosophy. FEE also publishes books, conducts seminars, and sponsors a network of discussion clubs to improve understanding of the principles of a free and prosperous society.

FEE is a non-political, non-profit 501(c)(3) tax-exempt organization, supported solely by private contributions and sales of its literature.

For further information, please contact:

The Foundation for Economic Education, Inc.
30 South Broadway
Irvington-on-Hudson, NY 10533
Telephone: (914) 591-7230
Fax: (914) 591-8910
E-mail: freeman@westnet.com